Will Smith

Will Smith is one of the most in-demand and respected stand-up comedians and writers in Britain, who won the 2004 *Time Out* Award for Outstanding Achievement in Comedy and the 2005 Chortle Award for Best Headliner. He is a regular panellist on Radio 4 shows such as *Banter*, *The Personality Test* and the Sony award-winning *Charm Offensive* with Armando Iannucci, as well as presenting his own show, *The Tao of Bergerac*. He also co-wrote the acclaimed BBC2 show *Time Trumpet*, and appears in the multi-award-winning BBC sitcom *The Thick of It*, as inept Tory researcher Phil Smith.

Praise for Will Smith and *How to Be Cool*

'Faultless. Brilliant. Magnificent' *Observer*

'Smith's material is gold . . . Tear-jerkingly funny' *Metro*

'One of the most reliably excellent comedians' *Independent on Sunday*

'Not just the ultimate cool bible, but also the ultimate fashion accessory, for people who don't know what fashion is, or what to do with an accessory' Danny Wallace

'An extremely funny book that anyone who doesn't consider them-selves cool (i.e. all non-arseholes) will enjoy. Will Smith will show you how to put the effort into "effortless poise"' David Mitchell

'Will Smith is the coolest guy in the world (if uncool is the new cool) – he's also terrifically funny' Harry Enfield

How To Be Cool

My Journey from Loser to Schmoozer

Will Smith

JOHN MURRAY

First published in Great Britain in 2007 by John Murray (Publishers)
An Hachette UK Company

First published in paperback in 2009

1

A CIP catalogue record for this title is available from the British Library

ISBN 978-0-7195-2001-3

Typeset in Rotis Semi Serif by Hewer Text UK Ltd, Edinburgh

Printed and bound by Clays Ltd, St Ives plc

John Murray policy is to use papers that are natural, renewable
and recyclable products and made from wood grown in sustainable
forests. The logging and manufacturing processes are expected to
conform to the environmental regulations of the country of origin.

John Murray (Publishers)
338 Euston Road
London NW1 3BH

www.johnmurray.co.uk

For Anne, who makes me feel cool

CONTENTS

COOL PLACES TO SAY 'MENTION MY NAME'
restaurant, club, tailor's, jeweller's
UNCOOL PLACES TO SAY 'MENTION MY NAME'
strip club, brothel, abattoir or morgue

Introduction

Class

I have never been cool. Not by any accepted standard. For a start I am avowedly middle class. It is the uncoolest class. Working class is cool because it reeks of struggle and authenticity. Upper class is cool because it reeks of eccentricity and wealth. Stuck bang in the middle you're despised by both ends. So, although from almost every other viewpoint I am given a head start in life, when it comes to being cool I am starting way behind the blocks. But rather than frantically try and catch up, at most points in life I decided to run the other way.

Jersey

After being born in Winchester (which gave me a shot at passing myself off as upper class) and spending a few years in a village outside Durham (which gave me a shot at passing myself off as working class), we settled in Jersey (which confirms me as middle class with a hint of nouveau riche). It's where I went to school, it's where I think of as home. Over the years I have found that people who don't know the island stereotype it as a refuge for tax dodgers, Nazi collaborators and, more recently, child abusers. Not the coolest frame of reference with which to make new friends. For the record, we don't all live in tacky villas built from Nazi gold by child slaves.

The Playground

On Jersey I went to school at Victoria College. It's kind of a public school, but it has state funding so there are no fees in the sixth form. This is my futile attempt to make it sound less lofty than it is, basically, but it was the poshest school on the island. The overall standard of living in Jersey is unsurprisingly high, so it was always a bit galling to take grief from the kids from other schools for being stuck-up nancies etc. So I live on an uncool island, within which I go to the uncoolest school. And within that subset I am also uncool on account of my academic diligence and respect for rules. That makes me uncool squared. The hierarchy amongst the pupils can be broken down as follows:

- Hard Lads. Okay, looking back they may not have been that hard, certainly not by today's standards. The worst they might do is shoplift from the pick'n'mix counter at

Woolworths, or phone in a bomb scare to get out of a detention. These days they might actually plant a bomb in response to some unreasonable demand from a teacher, like suggesting they stop throwing knives into a desk.

- Sporty Boys. Some crossover with the hard lads here, but essentially they were just fit and good-looking and made up most of the sports teams. My main contact with them would be if any kind of ball came near me during a sports lesson or lunchtime game, at which point the exhortation 'Leave it!' would be yelled with blood-freezing invective. Fair enough. Any attempt on my behalf to kick or catch the ball would have resulted in ignominious failure. At worst, I would accidentally propel it somewhere inaccessible like a roof or road. At best (from the point of view of those playing the game), I would fail to make contact with it and possibly fall over in the process.

- Science Boys. Your standard-issue nerds, who seemed to have their own private language. They also lacked any kind of awareness or self-consciousness as to just how nerdy they were, possibly due to safety in numbers, possibly because they were missing the part of the brain that tells you it's bad to invent conversations between the items of your lunchbox using a robot voice.

- Geek Boys. Neither good at science nor sport nor social transgression they float around on the edges, clinging to popular culture as their life raft in this sea of confusion.

The playground would be demarcated by these groups, much like the exercise yard of a maximum-security prison. But without the possibility of Ross Kemp popping in for a chat. There could be some crossover. As mentioned, a Hard Lad might also be a Sporty Boy. A Science Boy might have an interest in, or in rare cases be able to play, a sport. Otherwise a strict cultural apartheid was observed. As you might expect I was a Geek Boy. Bottom of the food chain.

In the sixth form another group emerged, the prefects. I was chosen for this office. And I was supremely ineffective. It's uncool to be a prefect, but then to be unable to use my powers with any sort of impact or dignity is majorly pathetic. For a week I was in charge of boys eating their lunch indoors. All I had to do was to make sure they disposed of their litter. Which they did. By pelting it at me.

The Stage

For some reason the arts were covered by the Geeks. In spite of my shyness I harboured theatrical ambitions. I was some-what unsuccessful in this. My school theatrical career can be summed up by the following lines.

- Year: 1987. Play: Henry IV Part I. Role: Traveller 4. Lines: 'Lord preserve us!'
- Year: 1988. Play: Ross. Role: Aide-de-Camp. Lines: 'I have

an urgent message for the Colonel!'; 'I'm not sure, sir'; 'I'll just go and get him'; 'Yes'.
- Year 1989. Play: King Lear. Role: backstage manager. Lines: none.

I started slow with Traveller 4, before peaking with Aide-de-Camp and slumping to a backstage role.

The Music

Part of your cultural identity as a teenager is defined by the music you like. I had two passions – Dire Straits and Marillion. For those of you who draw a blank at those names, I reserve my pity. For those of you who raise a sneer, I reserve my wrath. It was tough being a fan back in the day. It's even tougher now. Uncoolness stalks these bands like age and obsolescence circle a decaying Kate Moss. But I defiantly present my defence.

Dire Straits, the case against: bland middle-of-the-road AOR.

Dire Straits, the case for: beautifully crafted melodies, haunting atmospheric cinematic backgrounds, superlative guitar work, deftly written character songs. Look beyond their past ubiquity and richness lies within.

Marillion, the case against: overblown, pretentious retro prog.

Marillion, the case for: they took the baton from Floyd, Tull, Genesis and Yes and carried it on from the eighties to the present. Ambitious, towering, emotional, complex and rewarding.

Anyway, not only did I like uncool bands, I was also in one. We were called Songvolution. I played keyboards. We used to wear costumes on stage. I definitely wore a kaftan at one gig, and I may have dressed as a drummer boy at another. I'm not sure. It could be a dream; it could be a repressed memory. People join bands for sex and drugs. I joined because my friend Patrick asked me to help out because he'd fired the keyboard player and the band was booked to audition for a slot at a local stadium show.

Okay, some background here. Jersey has a stadium: Springfield Stadium. The dictionary in my word processor defines 'Stadium' as follows

'Stadium', noun. A place where people watch sports or other activities, usually a large enclosed flat area surrounded by tiers of seats for spectators.

It fits that description. I wouldn't say it was 'surrounded by tiers of seats', but there are definitely seats at one end and a flat bit where they play football. So I'm in a band and we're on the bill for a stadium gig. Sounds pretty cool. We passed the audition, now we get to walk out onstage to a sea of adoring faces, hands held aloft clapping in time as they chant our name. The promoters said they'd only sold sixty or so tickets in advance but that there would be a guaranteed walk-up crowd of eight hundred or so. We were on second, which was appropriate as there were two people in the audience, if you didn't count the first band and the police-men standing round the edge of the pitch waiting to control this phantom eight-hundred-strong walk-up crowd.

Lord of the Rings

Here are some of the uncool things I did at school:

- Pluralised the word 'discus' to 'disci' at the end of a games lesson. I maintain this was for comic effect, but in truth I may have clutched at this as a defence after the event.
- Wore a vest under a games shirt. What can I say – it was an unusually cold summer's day. Anyway, it was noticed and for a mercifully short 72 hours I was known as 'Vestboy'.
- Had an intimate knowledge of *Lord of the Rings*.

A word about this last infraction of cool. Everyone loves *Lord of the Rings* now, thanks to Peter Jackson's masterful films, but back in the eighties it was a lonely torch to carry. My love of Tolkien made me very much feel like Aragorn in the guise of Strider – an outcast of kingly birth waiting to claim his realm. And I didn't stop at *Lord of the Rings* and *The Hobbit*. Oh no, I had *The Silmarillion, Unfinished Tales*, the biography, the letters, the encyclopaedias, the books of maps, the calendars. All of these in hardback as well as paperback, some in deluxe editions. I even had second-hand paperback versions of the books I already had because they had different covers. None of these tomes could be described as 'girl bait'. At one point I even joined the Tolkien Society before realising that learning Elvish and dressing as the characters might be a step too far. And one that could only be passed off as cool if you revealed that you were an agent who had gone undercover to expose extremist elements in the Tolkien fan fraternity. Which would be a tough one to pull off. You'd have to fake a threat first. Probably not worth the effort.

Star Wars

My other geek passion was *Star Wars*. Now you might say that *Star Wars* is the opposite of *Lord of the Rings* in terms of the position of cool it occupies. You could argue that they've swapped round, *Star Wars* now being incredibly uncool thanks to George Lucas stinking out cinemas with his execrable prequels, and Jackson's films reigning supreme as the pinnacle of cinematic art. Well, yes, when I was growing up, *Star Wars* was incredibly cool. It captured the imagination of a generation. But even given such a cool franchise, I managed to push it towards questionable behaviour. I did this by the following methods.

- I formed a *Star Wars* fan club. I was the president. I sent newsletters. There was a quiz. I issued passwords. Things like 'Chewie' or 'Uncle Owen'. I can't remember how exactly these passwords empowered the six or seven members I accrued.
- I recorded my own audiobook of Donald F. Glut's novelisation of *The Empire Strikes Back*.
- I made a replica of the Millennium Falcon cockpit from Lego.

This was all between the ages of seven and ten. Don't worry, I'm over it now. Although for my twenty-fifth birthday I did go to a *Star Wars* convention with my dad and best friend. And you know what, we had a brilliant day.

Girls

Another way my uncoolness manifested itself was my utter terror in the face of girls. I was immensely shy as a boy and saw any slip of emotion as handing ammunition to enemies capable of brutal mockery. It was an all-boys' school, but there were pupil exchanges for some lessons between our school and the equivalent girls' establishment. There was one girl who came over to take A level history in our class. Although I had a crush on her, my way of expressing this – whenever I walked in to find she was the only other one there – was to pretend I had forgotten something and turn tail, then wait around till there were other people in the room. Quite the Casanova.

Because opportunities for meeting girls were very limited lesson-wise, it fell to extra-curricular events to fulfil this. One such event was the 'BAYS' disco. BAYS stood for British Association of Young Scientists. You can imagine what a romantic hotbed that was. The only unsexier ways that acronym could work would be

- Bald Angry Yuppies Sing
- Bugs And Yoghurt Supper
- Buy A Yak Shit
- Baboon And Yeti Sex
- Bad Apes Yodel Sick
- Big Anal Yellow Sores
- Bone A Young Sasquatch

Ironically that last one is probably closest to the truth of the event. Anyway, the point is, I wasn't even cool enough to go to the BAYS disco. If you imagine uncoolness in terms of an evolutionary picture of man learning to walk upright, with

Johnny Depp on the right as the walking man, I'm somewhere to the left of the picture in a part of the evolutionary
chain they haven't illustrated, like a one-legged fish flapping
on the edge of the primordial soup.

Christmas Elf

In the Christmas holidays of 1984 I got a job working in
the record department of Boots. I had high hopes for this,
bearing in mind that in films everyone who works in a record
department is always cool. But they're not usually working in
the record department of a high-street chemist. And they
don't have to dress as an elf. Yes, an elf. Not the full tights-
and-curly-shoes-with-bells-on elf of a Disney Christmas
movie. Just a green tunic, red belt and red pointy hat.
But that's enough of an elf costume that you can't pass
it off as a new look that will soon be sweeping the land. You
can't say, 'The joke's on you, loser: green is in!' I should point
out that I wasn't flying solo on this, it wasn't a unilateral
decision: the other male staff were wearing elf costumes, the
female staff were in Santa dresses. But still, when you're
thirteen and working in one of the three or four music outlets
on the island during the busiest retail week of the year, that's
a lot of ducking behind counters to avoid people you know.
Of course the inevitable happened, I was spotted. What
happened then was less inevitable. What would you do if

you saw a friend in an elf costume just at the start of his adolescent self-consciousness? Maybe have a joke and invent a nickname? Par for the course. My friend and now writing partner Roger Drew decided that the only decent course of action was to bring in all the girls he knew (at that point in his life about five including his mother and sister) to point and laugh from a distance. I still have the costume. And one day I will find a cool use for it that will square that particular circle. God knows what. Maybe if I save someone drowning wearing it. But that's a lot of hanging round weirs and rivers dressed as an elf. And what if instead of saving someone from drowning, I end up drowning myself? Great funeral oration – 'he died as he lived, dressed as an elf'.

Religious Knowledge

On Friday afternoons at school, fourth years and above were allowed to take part in activities other than lessons. You could join the CCF (College Cadet Force) which involved wearing a different uniform (green for army, blue for air force, navy for navy) and then being made to do lots of press-ups or crawl through a bog. I forget the details, but that's roughly what seemed to happen, and needless to say, it didn't appeal. You could sign up for various other activities, though – you could learn to sail, you could go and paint watercolours, you could help do up a car, you could even join a board-game group. Given my uncool ranking so far you might be forgiven for thinking that the board-game group is where I laid my hat, and that that hat would have been one with fake seagull shit and the logo 'Damn seagulls' on it (this is the uncoolest hat I can think of as it encourages people to think that the wearer knowingly retains shit on his head). Well, you'd be wrong. There was one rung lower than the board-game group, and that was the religious knowledge group. Not a group of people who wanted to hook up and read the Bible, although that would be uncool enough. No, this was for people who wanted to take an O Level in religious knowledge. That's right, ladies, I volunteered for extra divinity exams. Anyway, I got an A so you can all piss off.

Guns

Guns are not cool, let's make that clear. But so many of our cool cultural icons – James Bond, Indiana Jones, the Terminator – use them. It's very confusing. That is my defence for getting into rifle shooting. I joined the St Helier Small-bore Rifle Club. I was pretty good: I still have a target somewhere on which I scored a straight 100. Maybe I was doing it as some boost to my fragile masculinity, shattered by my appearance as a Christmas elf; I don't know. That theory was certainly rammed home to me after we won an inter-parish competition and our photo was on the back page of the local paper. The next day my English teacher kept repeating the phrase 'Small-bore' with exactly the right emphasis to make me feel I was compensating for some real or perceived under-endowment. I had succeeded at a sport, and a sport in which the phallic symbolism was unavoidable. That should transform me into the coolest dickswinger in town. But no, I'm still a nerd.

Things So Uncool I Blanked Them Out

By far and away the uncoolest thing I ever did growing up was to exhibit my cat in the Jersey Cat Club. I really had blanked this out, then came across an old A4 envelope stuffed with rosettes. Twiki (my cat named after Buck Rogers' robot) did pretty well – Best Non-Pedigree Cat in Show, no less. There were also photos of me with some trophies. I swear to you, I just don't know what I was thinking.

I also found a framed certificate from the 'Jersey Schools Science Fair'. My entry entitled 'Rockpool' won 'First Prize' with 'Distinction'. What is uncooler – the fact I won a science prize with some seashells, or the fact that I had it framed? Or the fact that I've still got it and it hangs in my kitchen.

The other thing I came across was a letter from Margaret Thatcher thanking me for my letter of support. It appears I wrote to her congratulating her on her 1987 election victory. What a little twat.

University

University. A chance to cut loose and enjoy life. Spread your wings, go a little crazy. I was at university in Southampton. At the time of my attendance it was famous for two things

- Benny Hill
- The Titanic

I don't think I need add anything more. It's not a particularly cool city, and my route towards it was not particularly cool. It was the only university to offer me a place. I was rejected by about fourteen universities. I applied in my last year of school, got nothing, went through clearing, decided to take a year off and reapply, got one offer. This in spite of my excellent academic record, glowing references and high exam results – 5 As and 7 Bs at O level which is the equivalent of a Nobel Prize at GCSE, and 1 A and 2 Bs at A level. Again, compared to today's exams that pretty much makes me Einstein. So I ended up at Southampton, the sole plus of which was its proximity to the New Forest. I like woods and the novels of Thomas Hardy. Yes, I know, I am uncool.

So what do most people do at university? They get drunk

and have lots of sex. And in between they get a degree. Or, like me, they read a lot of books, drink a total of three pints and have no sex whatsoever.

Oh God, I've just had a flashback. I think as part of giving myself a new quirky identity I used a canvas bag with a cat on it for the first few weeks. Yes, I think I did. Excuse me, I have to go and sit in a dark room for a few minutes.

London

'When a man is tired of London, he is tired of life.' So said Samuel Johnson. He didn't add that that man might also be tired of overcrowding, rats, random violence and a high concentration of arseholes in the Camden and Shoreditch areas. London is where I bought my first flat. Pretty cool. I had a flat-warming party. It felt pretty cool playing host. People complimented me on the unexpectedly spacious hall, the garden and the décor. I felt quite the dashing bachelor. Then someone noticed that in the kitchen there was a clip on the wall by the sink, hanging from which was a pair of washing-up gloves. A question was asked – was this clip there when I bought the flat? If I could go back in time and give my past self but one piece of advice, it would be this: deny you bought a clip with which to hang up your washing-up gloves. In fact, don't even answer the question verbally, simply rip the clip from the wall and grind it under your heel whilst laughing at the preposterous nature of the enquiry. But no, without thinking I admitted to the purchase.

The mood changed. Not in that instantly chilling 'stranger walks into a pub of locals' way. Or the way it might change at a wedding if, due to an unfortunate acoustic, your whispered 'Christ she looks fat' were to echo round the church. It was more that a seed had been sowed. A seed of doubt. A doubt that said, 'Maybe Will isn't as cool as he seems. Maybe he's not a young cool bachelor, but a slightly odd creepy single man.' There was an awkward pause, which I put down to the natural rhythm of a party. There will always be those sudden silences, and as long as you cover them by opening another packet of cashews, all will be well. Except now all I could hear was the sound of me opening some cashews – the tear of the plastic, the tinkle of the nuts cascading into the bowl and then the simple question.

Why did you buy a clip for your washing-up gloves?

I didn't quite know how to answer this. I knew the answer of course – to hang them up with so that they dry away from the bowl and to avert the accompanying risk that they fall into the bowl – and/or between the bowl and the sink – where there might be remaining water which could not only prevent the drying of the exterior but also potentially find its way inside the glove. Isn't that obvious? I hesitated. Maybe it was a trick question? Like in police interviews where they disorientate a suspect by obsessing about how they tie their laces or aggressively quiz them about their favourite type of orange. But the person posing the question was not a police officer, and I was not a suspect. So I answered truthfully.

To hang them up with.

I decided that although this was obvious, it must be one of those moments where someone has drawn a blank. Like when you stop a waiter to ask him where the loo is, only to have him indicate the door you're standing in front of with the word 'Toilet' written on it. I had stated the obvious at the instigation of my enquirer who would now give one of those 'Silly me, what an idiot' laughs and the conversation could get back to what a good investment I'd made in an upcoming area with some really cool ethnic restaurants.

Why do you need to hang them up?

I laughed and looked around, expecting everyone else to join in with me at mocking this parvenu, this man who clearly didn't have an adult kitchen of his own, who knew nothing of the pressures and strains and duties of cooking and cleaning, and the resultant importance of having dry gloves. The support was not forthcoming. Neither was my answer.

But the expressions around me told me an answer was clearly expected, so I obliged.

To dry them.

But they're waterproof.

A laugh from the assembled. Who the hell does he think he is? In fact, who the hell is he? I don't recognise him! What is he doing at my flat-warming party? I work out that he's the new boyfriend of a friend of mine. He should shut up and play the game: namely, don't come in here, drink my beer and eat my nuts and dips and then try and ridicule me. That won't play, compadre. You're on my turf, and those are my gloves you're mocking. How about I knock you down with a little cold, hard truth!

If you leave them over the sink they can fall in and get wet inside. It's actually quite a good idea.

I start talking with all the confidence and attack of a Spearmint Rhino regional manager telling assembled stag parties that the PA's blown so there'll be no dancing tonight but free drinks vouchers can be collected at the bar. Conversation breaks out around me. My attacker smirks off. I go round checking everyone is all right for drinks and Pringles and can't wait for everyone to leave so I can draw a picture of him on a pillow and punch it till I pass out. Afterwards, tidying up, I swear I find fragments of my ego on the floor.

Turning It Around

Somehow I managed to turn some of my uncoolness to my advantage. Many of my uncool exploits have fuelled my stand-up routines. In fact a friend of mine recently remarked that it was as if I had purposefully lived my early years in a state of perpetual uncool so as to reap the artistic rewards later. Thank God I am such an obsessive self-archivist. Other people might wish they had got rid of their cat club rosettes, allowing total denial. Not me, I see them as props. I toured a successful show about my obsession with Marillion that featured filmed appearances with original lead singer, Fish. And I made a Radio 4 show that was Jersey-tinged featuring as it did the voice of John Nettles and also my party piece, '6 Degrees of Bergerac'. A few years earlier my dad had alerted me and my writing partner to the fact that the BBC was repeating *Bergerac* in the afternoons. As a) he is of a kindly disposition and b) he had recently retired and was looking for things to do, he began videoing the show and sending it over to us. In work breaks we would watch episodes for nostalgia value, and also for hilarity at the creakiness of some of the plots. There will usually be a shady company or individual who Bergerac investigates only to discover at some point that they are a division of 'Hungerford Enterprises'; cue a scene with Bergerac's canary-yellow-slack-wearing cigar-chomping ex-father-in-law to explain the plot. As these breaks started getting longer and longer we started to get guiltier and guiltier at the work we weren't doing. All of that slacking was instantly justified when one of us suggested that given the large number of guest stars in the show who had gone on to even greater things, you could probably connect any film to *Bergerac*. It fell to me as the more anal and obsessive half of the partnership to investigate this. Which I did over a week's holiday in Italy with my then girlfriend. Many people would be happy to partake of scenery, food and wine with their partner. I preferred to go through reams and reams of printouts from the Internet Movie Database, writing out flow charts of actors and films all leading back to specific episodes of *Bergerac*, then commit it to memory. It can be done, and I am the only person to do it. This has made me slightly cool. Certainly for the first five minutes after someone discovers my gift. For those five minutes they are amazed at the speed and range of my recall, other people are beckoned over to challenge me, incredulity mounts. Then the atmosphere changes slightly and I am regarded with something between the irritation one feels at a cricket or football bore, and the frostiness a detective might develop when in the cellar of someone he suddenly suspects might be a serial killer. Still, for five minutes I am the coolest person in the room, which is a long way from where I started.

It might seem slightly self-defeating to have as an intro-duction for a book called *How To Be Cool*, this litany of uncool confessions. Well, the purpose of the introduction is twofold.

1) To bolster the confidence of the reader. Whoever is reading this, I think you will agree, you are already cooler than me.
2) To show that it's never too late, and that with coolness, the pendulum swings inexorably. Just as a s`opped clock is right twice a day, we all have our moments.

So there you go. This book won't really tell you how to be cool, but it will hopefully make you laugh at the absurd lengths that some people go to attain coolness.

P.S. I have avoided that thing authors do when they write a new introduction which is to put the date and place where they're writing it. It might seem cool, but it isn't. It's actually quite boastful. How irritating is this?

Will Smith, September 2008, the Bahamas

Very, is the answer. I don't want my nose rubbed in it as to how glamorous an author's life is! I want to be made to feel better about my own.

Will Smith, September 2008, a skip in East London

Chapter 1
AN ANALYSIS OF COOL

What is Cool?

Cool is the aura of confidence, the perfume of success, the fuel of popular culture. We all want it, but can we get it?

You might think, no, I can never be as cool as Cary Grant. Well, the good news is, you can. This book will transform you from a lumbering hulk whose appearance provokes the rolling of eyes to the sort of person who demands attention. From John McCririck to Johnny Depp, all it takes is a mindset, and it all flows.

In many ways, it's a lot easier now than it has ever been. That's because most people in this country are deeply uncool. We dress badly, most of us are alcoholics, a lot of us are overweight, and there's a general celebration of ignorance and a frowning at knowledge and talent. It really is a cool buyer's market out there. This country is crying out for a return to sophistication, and this book aims to help with this.

A lot of people mistake cool for rebelliousness. It's so much more than that. People who break the rules for the sake of it are seeking attention, striving to be different: it's a contrivance. Cool people don't really care what other people think of them; they're following their cool muse. So some elements of cool must be unique to you. Just don't make it a trilby with a playing card tucked in the band.

And let's not forget that what is cool is open to debate. Cast your mind back a decade or so to the 'Cool Britannia' movement. Cool then, but looking back now, it all seems slightly embarrassing. Its main proponent was Liam Gallagher, a man who walks like he woke up in a peat bog. And it generally featured musicians so forgettable that even they can't remember the name of the band they were in.

But even if you transcend your own time to ascend to the pantheon of cool, a close inspection can puncture your aura. Even the coolest people have their weak spots. Let's look at some of the men and women considered the coolest. We have:

ELVIS PRESLEY
COOL SIDE – Merged blues, country, hillbilly and bluegrass to bring rock'n'roll to the masses. Looked beautiful, was sexually magnetic, and seen as dangerous by conservative America.

UNCOOL SIDE – Died on the toilet straining to pass an impacted, clay-like substance in his colon brought on by a highly calorific diet of fried food, in turn undertaken due to crushing loneliness resulting from the isolation of fame and an exhausting touring schedule.

MADONNA

COOL SIDE – Sexually empowered megastar in complete control of her career, always at cutting edge of contemporary pop stylings.

UNCOOL SIDE – Terrible actress, whiney voice that can warp metal.

JOHNNY CASH

COOL SIDE – Dressed in black, straight walking, straight talking.

UNCOOL SIDE – Only knew about three chords.

JAMES DEAN

COOL SIDE – Looked amazing, had edgy, dangerous air.

UNCOOL SIDE – Performed homosexual acts in return for Hollywood contacts.

MARLON BRANDO

COOL SIDE – Smouldered as Johnny in *The Wild One*, the face of rebelliousness for a generation.

UNCOOL SIDE – Got really, really fat. By the end he would have been too big to make it as a Rik Waller lookalike.

JACK KEROUAC

COOL SIDE – Invented Beat writing and was one of the catalysts for 60s counterculture.

UNCOOL SIDE – Is a rubbish writer who couldn't work out a train timetable and so ended up bumming round America.

BOB DYLAN

COOL SIDE – Voice of a generation, prolific writer of songs with the depth of poetry and literature, follows his muse regardless of audience reaction.

UNCOOL SIDE – Sang like a tramp at Live Aid.

When they're in the zone, what do they have that makes them cool? It's the detachment, the hint of danger, the sense that they're dancing to the beat of their own drum. So part of it is about being yourself. Don't follow the herd! That doesn't mean being contrary for the sake of it, or being a killjoy. It just means not thinking that the best thing you can do with your hard-earned free time is to drink as much as you can, vomit in the street and then have sex with whatever is to hand.

COOL PETS
Dog, cat, tropical fish
UNCOOL PETS
Rat, tapeworm, midget

How Do You Become Cool?

The question is – how do you become cool? There are degrees of cool. Not many people can be as cool as Frank Sinatra, as part of being cool is being an individual: it can't be copied wholesale. If it is, it doesn't quite work. Frank is undoubtedly cool. An overweight man in his sixties sweating his way through a pub karaoke version of 'My Way', which in his case means two failed marriages and a GBH charge, isn't.

Also, what's cool can change over time. The Fonz was cool when he starred in a 70s sitcom set in the 50s. It's a peculiar filter. If you behaved like the Fonz now – hanging out with kids who are still at school, beckoning them into the men's room for 'chats', etc. – it wouldn't be quite so cool.

So a large part of it is being true to yourself. That's why Stephen Fry is as cool as John Lydon. They're both individuals.

Now, there's your outward cool, which consists of modes of behaviour etc., but there's also your inner cool, your self-image. And, in your own head, you can get away with whatever you want in order to help you feel cool. Often you'll find that there is no actual cool to be gained from a situation, but you just have to play it that way in your head. If you want to imagine yourself as a futuristic road warrior – leather trench coat, steel helmet, cigar lit from match scratched on your boot heel or stubbled chin, then go for it. Just don't actually do it. Unless you're going to a fancy dress party. Or if there has actually been a nuclear war and you're now stalking the burned-out cities looking for the last humans on earth, in which case, all bets are off.

Han Solo vs. Luke Skywalker: A Case Study in Cool

The original *Star Wars* films are amongst the coolest films ever made. Let's not count the prequels, though, which are amongst the uncoolest films ever made. *The Phantom Menace* starts with some kind of union dispute. Yeah, 'cause what the kids wanted was *Star Wars* plus plotlines revolving around industrial action. But the originals – Ewoks aside – are unquestionably brilliant. What's fascinating is that the character George Lucas clearly sees as the focal point of the films, Luke Skywalker, is deeply uncool. Whereas Han Solo, a supporting character, is just about the coolest guy to ever wear a waistcoat. Here are the things that are cool about Han Solo:

1 He wins fights
2 He has a swaggering walk
3 He wears cool clothes
4 Against their better judgement, women want him
5 He's a top pilot
6 He owns the fastest ship in the galaxy – a hotrod, basically
7 His best friend is a Wookie

And here are the things that are uncool about Luke Sky-walker:

1 He usually loses light sabre fights, then has a sulk
2 He bounces around like a puppy waiting to be toilet trained
3 He wears a judo outfit in the first film, an orange American prisoner outfit in the second, and belatedly attempts to look cool in black in the third
4 He fancies his sister for a bit
5 He needs an old man's ghost to help him fly
6 He has the spaceship equivalent to a Ford Mondeo
7 His best friend is a gay robot

Here's the interesting thing – when did Han Solo stop being cool? When he became pussy-whipped. Up until *Return Of The Jedi*, Han was a rebel, a rogue, looking out for number one, and arrogant when it came to the effect of his charms upon women. His exchange with Princess Leia – 'I love you!', 'I know' – is one of the coolest lines in cinema history. A whole generation of boys went 'Yes! I want to be like him!' Then, once he gets the girl and commits to the Rebellion, he becomes really dull. There's no edge, no danger, no doubt as to the course of his actions. Now Han always does the right thing, but before you felt like it was a struggle, like he was making a choice. How much cooler is it to overcome temptation than to simply never experience it? There's a lesson for us all – do the right thing, but never make yourself out to be a pushover. A bit of demon-wrestling never hurts when it comes to your state of cool. As long as it's not a massive scary demon, e.g. 'It takes every ounce of my self-control not to follow strangers home and mark their territory with my musk.'

> Unless you are a Musketeer or Victorian engineer, it is uncool to have a waxed moustache

Coolest Cultural Icon – James Bond?

It's hard to think of a cooler figure in Western culture than James Bond. How come an assassin with commitment issues is cool? He's on a government salary, it's not even like he's pulling in a million a hit. What makes James Bond cool? Well, he

- Dresses well
- Has a signature drink
- Wins fights
- Beds lots of women

- Has a healthy disregard for authority
- Has maverick tendencies
- Can drive cars, boats and planes at high speed
- Knows his way around a casino

In many ways, James Bond is a blueprint for masculine cool. There are further nuances of cool within his many incarnations.

SEAN CONNERY

He's cool in his eighties, so of course he was cool back then. Looks cool, moves cool, sounds cool. A Zen Master of Cool.

GEORGE LAZENBY

Quit after one film thinking he was too big a star for the role. Became an estate agent. Definitely not cool.

ROGER MOORE

Cool at first, but later films where he beds women a third of his age, with his chestnut-dyed hair and liver-spotted hands, are a bit creepy, especially in conjunction with lines like 'I'm an early riser myself' and 'I tossed and turned but got off eventually'.

TIMOTHY DALTON

Probably cooler as Prince Barin in the 1980 version of *Flash Gordon*. Barin is sardonic, a rebel, likes a bad girl in spite of himself, can fight, and comes good in the end. He also administers a mercy killing to *Blue Peter*'s Peter Duncan – cool!

PIERCE BROSNAN

Pierce looks cool, and has a really cool run. The uncoolest thing about his reign was the CGI surf sequence in *Die Another Day*, which looks like it was done on a ZX Spectrum.

DANIEL CRAIG

Well, he *seems* to be the coolest since Sean. But I don't care what anyone says, those trunks looked ridiculous. They're the sort of trunks men used to wear in the 70s that had a little pocket with a zip.

Chapter 2
THE BASICS OF COOL

Is it Cool to Smoke?

We all know that smoking looks cool. Obviously, the image you give off depends on what you're smoking.

- Cigarette: musician, writer, artist, poet, private detective
- Roll-ups: student, graduate who still wishes they were a student, jazz fan
- Cigar: mogul, Mafia boss, someone who is generally untrustworthy in business
- Pipe: Victorian detective, Norwegian whaler, shepherd

And it has a certain coolness in the statement it makes – 'I know this could give me and those around me a hideous disease resulting in a painful and premature death, but you know what, I live for the moment.' It's like riding a bike without a helmet or fluorescent stripes. And now, with the UK-wide ban, you can be even more of a rebel! Skulk outside in the rain like an investigative reporter muttering 'Goddamn Nanny State wanna control my life! I say screw the corporations! Except the tobacco ones!'

UNCOOL REASONS TO BE THROWN OUT
OF A CLUB

Pickpocketing, marking your territory, being Paul
Danan

Is It Cool to Drink?

Our culture has a strange relationship with drink. In fiction,
alcoholics are really cool. They're poets and musicians. In
reality, they're tramps, or men whose wives have left them,
and they're generally depressing to be with. So a drink
problem is definitely not cool. It's cool if you can hold your
drink, though, as long as you're in control. If it gets to the
stage of beer on your cornflakes or minesweeping from cans
in bins, then you've got a problem, which is uncool. But it's
also uncool if you can't hold your drink. If this is the case,
and you know you get drunk too quickly, or throw up after
two pints, then think of a really good excuse. Such as

- 'I'm allergic to alcohol'
- 'I'm in training for the marathon'
- 'I'm on a detox diet that I will only break for vintage
  champagne'

Don't, whatever you do, say

- 'It makes me wee too much'
- 'It makes me express opinions on race that are considered unacceptable in a modern society'
- 'You want to see what it does to me? Bring it on, arsehole! But right now this is like Bruce Banner warning you, you are going to get Hulked!'

Of course, drinking is cool, but it depends on the context. It's cool to drink in a bar, restaurant, club or at home. The following locations are not so cool:

- During a church service
- In the toilets at work
- In the reception at the doctors, dentist or of general offices
- In court
- In the delivery room
- At an inquest
- At an autopsy

So pick the place carefully, as there's a standard social contract about where it's acceptable to drink. But then pick the drink and the amount. There's a more detailed analysis of this in later chapters. But, basically, it's cool up to the point you're sick on your shoes and can't remember trying to dry-hump the fruit machine.

Is it Cool to Break the Law?

Well, this depends on the crime. Five miles over the speed limit, that shows boldness, virility and power. The smuggling of fissile material from former Eastern Bloc states is cool in a Tom Clancy book, but terrifying in reality. Likewise, fraud is cool in popular culture – films like *Ocean's 11* and TV shows like *Hustle* propagate the myth that con artists are always cool or loveable, and only target people who deserve to be ripped off – when, of course, the reality is that most con artists are scum who steal the life savings of confused old women by pretending to be from the Gas Board. A flirtation with crime is cool. Look at rappers. Having been shot at or having been a gang member, drug dealer or pimp immediately confers a level of cool. Same with Mafia figures. We'd all secretly like to know one, so that, if someone keys our car or burgles us, say, there'll be an avenging angel to shake down the local crims and ensure the return of our goods. This is all fine from a distance, but up close no one really wants to be associated with someone who can make a body disappear. So play it loose and cool – your views happen to coincide with the law, that's why you follow it.

> **UNCOOL NAMES TO DROP**
>
> Jodie Marsh, Alastair Stewart, a Kemp (Martin or Ross), Haddaway, Yazz, Himmler

Is it Cool to Break the Rules?

Absolutely. 'Rules' are for deadheads, squares and 'The Man'. That said, it depends on the specific rule you are infringing. When you're fourteen, it's really cool to disregard the 'no bombing' rule at the local swimming pool. In your forties, it looks a little bit desperate. Expect people to ask you where your carer is. Here are some rules you can break for cool:

- Two schoolchildren at a time in the shop
- Keeping feet off seats on buses and trains, etc.
- Keeping behind the yellow line at passport control

And here are some rules, the breaking of which will cause you untold problems:

- Don't touch the dancers
- No shoes in the mosque
- Don't goose the bouncers

How to Have Cool Hobbies

We all know the uncool ones – trainspotting, battle re-enacting, running a Michael Ball fan club. But can you have a cool one? Isn't the word 'hobby' itself deeply uncool? Well, it does smack of model railways and the 50s, but there are some pretty cool extra-curricular activities you can undertake.

- Musical instruments. Always cool, especially if you study them for years without telling anyone, then wow them with a virtuoso display and claim you've only been learning a couple of months.
- Writing can be cool. Make sure it's something uncommercial, so no one need see your efforts, lest they be wanting. No one publishes poetry, for instance, but if you say you write plays, films or novels, after a while people will expect to see them produced or published, otherwise they will think you are a fantasist, or crap.
- Linguist. Being able to speak several languages is very cool. That said, it depends on your reasons for learning them. Great if it's for reading novels in their original languages, travel or even business. Less cool if it's as part of your educative programme designed to help you re-break the Enigma Code.
- Mountain climbing. It's physical; it's to do with challenging yourself and celebrating the awesomeness of nature. And it means you'll be able to do every position in the book.
- Ice climbing. Another cool one, it's a more exotic version of mountain climbing. Be careful, though, if you push it beyond any of the last few physical pursuits listed, it

veers perilously close to survivalism, which, Ray Mears aside, is practised by mentalists.

How to Have a Cool DVD Collection

The following must never appear on your shelves:

- *Police Academy 1–6*
- *Beastmaster 1–3*
- *Highlander 1–5*
- *Confessions Of A Window Cleaner*
- Anything with Steven Seagal or Jean-Claude Van Damme

If you must have these titles, hide them from polite company. But be warned, their discovery will be more embarrassing than if it was pornography. Fill your shelves with works by Scorsese, Kieslowski, Herzog, Truffaut, Gilliam and Fellini. The closest you go to mainstream is Spielberg, Lean and Scott (Ridley, not Tony). You're allowed a few wildcards, obviously. But stick to the list and you'll draw the sort of admiring glances that *Maniac Cop* really couldn't provide.

How to Have a Cool CD Collection

This advice also goes for your iPod. Hide the following and their ilk:

- T'Pau
- Meatloaf
- Bryan Adams
- Falco
- Boyzone
- Ronan Keating
- Lighthouse Family
- The Fat Boys
- German Drinking Songs of the 30s

And make sure you've got some Beatles, Stones, Miles Davis and a bit of classical, then fill in the gaps. Always have the hottest band from each era, e.g. U2, Oasis, The Arctic Monkeys, but only the first album. Then go on about how they sold out, never lived up to their promise, Joe Strummer's the only man who kept his integrity, etc. And remember that eclecticism is cool and so is a bit of idiosyncrasy – for instance, you could get away with one Iron Maiden album, or a staunch defence of the song-writing skills of Neil Diamond. But not the complete works of Daniel O'Donnell. Which leads us neatly on to the next item . . .

Can You Be Cool When you Love Something Generally Considered Terrible?

I'm not talking about a love of bird cruelty, or breaking into women's homes to steal underwear. I mean, what if you really love Def Leppard? What if the electric harmonies of 'Animal', or the industrial groove of 'Pour Some Sugar On Me', or even the haunting ballad beat of 'Hysteria' itself makes you really happy? Do you live a lie? Why should you be made to feel bad by other people's judgement as to what is considered 'good' music? Surely there's no good music or bad music, there's just music? Well, there are some things that really cross the line into uncool. In fact, they don't just cross it, they keep running till the line is completely out of sight. They include the covers albums by the following:

- Ian McShane
- Brian Conley
- Mike Reid
- Vinnie Jones

As well as the following genres:

- White reggae
- Classical music played on synthesisers
- Military marches

And the following artists:

- Kenny G

But cool is also about being an individual, not going with the herd. Here are some musicians and genres not considered cool, but a persistent liking for them may confer cool upon you:

- Mark Knopfler – great guitarist, wonderful songwriter. The Killers love him, they covered 'Romeo and Juliet', so rehabilitation is not without hope.
- Progressive Rock – the problem with Punk is it allowed you to be in a band without being able to play an instrument particularly well. We don't put up with this kind of amateurism when it comes to people representing our country at sport, or with people who work in the healthcare profession, so why should it be any different with music? The members of Yes are all brilliant instrumentalists: this is a good thing. Ian Anderson from Jethro Tull plays the flute! These guys go against the grain, so aren't they just the teensiest bit cool?
- Country Music – Johnny Cash is one of the coolest men to ever walk the face of the earth. If country music is good enough for him, it's good enough for the rest of us. Just avoid crazy-looking men in spurs singing songs backing increased US military involvement overseas.

The liking of an unpopular or much-dismissed band or singer shows strength of character. There is cool to be had in idiosyncrasy. Just pick your musician carefully. It just can't be done with Chesney Hawkes, no matter how hard you argue that 'The One And Only' isn't really representative of his body of work.

> **COOL FIRST DATES**
> Restaurant, theatre, gig
> **UNCOOL FIRST DATES**
> Regional darts contest, falconry display, cage fighting

How to Like Cool Television Programmes

There was a time, not so long ago, when it was cool to say 'I don't watch television', to not even have a set. No longer. Partly because of the ubiquitous onward march of a Western global television culture. You could ignore it when it was four channels, you could ignore it when it was five channels. In fact, even then, it still felt like four. But now there's a profusion of channels, to ignore it seems wilfully stuck in the past. Even if you hate it, you still have to engage with it. The other reason you should have an opinion on television is that some of it is unarguably brilliant. It's best to namecheck quality American drama – *The Sopranos, The West Wing, The Shield, The Wire, Deadwood*. Watch these and then you can legitimately say things like 'With *The Wire*, television has finally reached the depth of reality achieved by the great Victorian novelists', '*The Sopranos* is the West laid bare' and '*Deadwood* shows the birth of America in microcosm', and not only will you sound cool, you won't sound like a tosser. That's only been possible in the last ten years. Before then, television – shows like *I, Claudius* and *Edge Of Darkness* aside – was crap. You'd never hear people saying 'My God, did you see *The Rockford Files* last night!' or 'I like to tape a whole series of *Juliet Bravo* and then watch it all at once over a weekend!' Stick with those shows and you will always sound cool. Just avoid the following. If you like them, as with a fondness for David Cameron, never admit to it in public.

- *100 Greatest Things*
- ITV2's *Dancing On Ice: Defrosted*
- Any of the myriad National Lottery quizzes. For Christ's sake, just tell us the fucking numbers!

Can A Politician Be Cool?

Well, there's JFK. He was young, dynamic and stylish. But more importantly, he slept with Marilyn Monroe. Other than that, the list runs a bit short . . . Tony Blair for a bit? He used to be in a band, he liked REM, he came across as relaxed, reasonable and focussed. But the whole false 45 minute claim/mishandling of Iraq war/cash for peerages scandal takes the sheen off a bit. For any politicians reading this book, here are some tips:

- Never, ever try to namedrop a band unless you're sure you've got the name right. They'll know you're lying if you say something like 'I'm a big fan of the Kaiser Chieftains!' or 'I dig the Coldplay group'.
- If you're photographed with a bunch of people who work in a supermarket, try not to look like you'll want to wash after shaking hands with them.
- Allow yourself to take style tips, but only to improve your existing look. You could probably get a better-cut jacket, and buy some decent shirts and jeans that actually fit. But don't start dressing like you're off to a Mighty Boosh gig.

Things That Might Seem Cool but Actually Aren't

1 Singing to a woman as you walk up to her in a bar. Like most things Tom Cruise does, that scene from *Top Gun* now has a very creepy edge.

2 Wearing a brimmed hat. This is only acceptable if you are one of the following:
   - A cowboy
   - A shepherd
   - An eccentric old musician gentleman from Mexico or Cuba
   - A member of U2 during the *Joshua Tree* era
   - Indiana Jones

   Otherwise it's too much of a statement.

3 Constantly making and giving out mix CDs. It basically says 'I've got all these amazing tracks by bands you'd never come across in your dull, pedestrian lives. Thank God for me, otherwise you'd be stuck listening to the Stones and the Eagles!' Well, a) there's nothing wrong with the Stones and the Eagles, and maybe they've sold a lot because people like them. And b) most music can now be readily accessed via websites. So hopefully people who go around handing out copies of CDs by bands who do less good versions of stuff that everyone already knows will be a thing of the past. 'They're like a lo-fi Velvet Underground!' 'I have The Velvet

Underground, they are lo-fi enough. Now please leave me alone.'

4 Wearing a kilt at a wedding. Now this is fine if you're the groom and you have some vague Scottish ancestry. But not if you're one of those blokes other people refer to as 'a joker', 'a real live wire' or 'the life and soul of the party'. Forget it. In reality, you're like Gazza – a chronic alcoholic surrounding yourself with noise and energy to drown out the roaring silence that suffocates your soul.

5 Drinking at breakfast. You may as well live on a bench.

6 Playing loud music from a car. Obviously this is some kind of virility statement. No one needs to hear music so loud that your joints dislocate. Well, if you look at people's faces as you drive by, you'll see that they don't think you're cool. Their expression tends to be 'Oh for God's sake, give it a rest!' Or 'At least play something good!' I agree, I don't think people would mind as much if Beethoven's use of Schiller's *Ode To Joy* at the climax of his ninth symphony was blaring out. Most people don't want to hear Christina Aguilera at most times of the day. And certainly not unasked for when they're trying to get to sleep for work and some arsehole's using her to make the windows rattle.

7 Driving a loud motorbike. Maybe you think that, by doing that, people are going to go 'Hey, do you reckon that's the Fonz?' But they don't. They tend to go 'I bet he's hung like an anchovy!' Which you probably are, otherwise

51

you wouldn't have a big piece of throbbing metal between our legs. Apparently *Newsnight*'s Peter Snow is hung like a hobbit's forearm. You never see him on a souped-up Kawasaki.

8 Hiring a white limo. Not film stars. Not rap stars. No, it's slags in a can.

9 Being able to put your fist in your mouth. Freak.

10 Having a threesome. Someone always gets benched.

Is it cool to invent an unusual Christian name for your child? No. Get a proper job, you've clearly got too much time on your hands

How to Cope With Someone Cooler Than You

The really cool person knows when to bow out gracefully. If you're at a party and Johnny Depp walks in, you just got beat. While he's talking about pirates being the first rock stars, don't say 'That's a bunch of crap! Pirates didn't have fans, people didn't turn up to see them recreate some of their best known boardings. And I can't imagine Westlife making everyone on a galleon walk the plank!' Right as you are, you will sour the mood. When someone hands him a guitar and he starts playing old gypsy melodies, don't whip out a Rubik's Cube and show the girls your moves. When he puts his hand on your girlfriend's rear, don't say 'Outside, *mano a mano*. No press, and no law.' Just say 'Be my guest. Mind if I watch? I could learn a few things.'

THE BASICS COOLOMETER TEST

1 You're in a no-smoking area when someone lights up. Do you

a) Hit them over the head with a fire extinguisher shouting 'Flamer!'

b) Point at your arse and yell 'How'd you like to breathe my butt fumes?!'

c) Point out the no-smoking law

d) Light the end of a biro and smoke it with them

2 You are flashed breaking the speed limit. Do you

a) Screech to a halt, torch the car and set off cross-country to a new life in the hills

b) Reverse back to the camera and wave a sign saying 'Please forgive me' quickly across the sensor in the hope it will trigger the camera

c) Slow your speed and resign yourself to paying a fine

d) Go to the nearest bar and ask 'Who's ready for some speed lovin'? This arse is wanted in five counties!'

3 **Someone at a party starts telling a story about how they saved some orphans from a burning building in Nepal. Do you**

a) Shake up a canned drink and then open it in their face, saying 'That would have put out the fire!'

b) Try to start a conga line

c) Nod along, looking concerned

d) Ask 'Were there any fit ones?'

4 **You arrive at an important social function slightly the worse for drink. Do you**

a) Start a food fight whilst singing Russ Abbot's 'Atmosphere'

b) Raise a toast to Oliver Reed, then drink till you forget your own name

c) Have some coffee and start drinking again at everyone else's pace

d) Go round explaining in a loud voice how 'I'm a little bit drunk', then segue into an angry defence of imperialism

5 Someone takes your iPod and mocks you for having Survivor's 'Eye of the Tiger'. Do you

a) Attempt to garrotte them with your headphone lead
b) Hold up your fists and snarl 'Say that again to Clubber Lang!'
c) Point out that, strange as it may seem, having that track on continuous play got you through the London Marathon
d) Sing the song whilst acting out key scenes from *Rocky 3*

If you answered mainly 'a', you're as cool as a newsreader at a breakdance competition. Loosen up, dog!

If you answered mainly 'b', you're kind of cool, but you have your weak points. Maybe you once went to see T'pau live, or use the chat-up line 'Tonight, is about tonight'.

If you answered mainly 'c', congratulations, you are cool! It's like Fonzie and Han Solo had a baby!

If you answered mainly 'd', oh dear, you're about as cool as a turd in a punchbowl.

Chapter 3
HOW TO BE COOL . . .
THE LOOK

A large part of being cool is visual. And I'm not talking about being fashionable. A truly cool look can transcend fashion: it's timeless, classic. You can't be a slave to fashion and still be cool – you're following instructions. All that shows is you have an ability to go 'I want to look like them', which in all likelihood is a look that can at best be described as 'twattish'.

How to Have Cool Clothes

Part of being cool is about confidence, daring to be different. This can be readily achieved with eccentric dress. But there are some absolute no-no's.

- A fake leopard-skin trilby. The sort of thing Will Young would wear on a T4 interview. Hideous.
- One glove. You might get away with it if you're Jean-Michel Jarre and you're playing a light harp, but only just.
- A bandana. OK on a rap star, and Steven Van Sandt from the E Street Band has worn us down. Everyone else, bar nineteenth-century Mexican revolutionaries, think again.

- A T-shirt with a tuxedo pattern. Simply no.
- A boiler suit and stilettos. Again, like the leopard-skin trilby, a look supported by the sort of airhead fame-slut who presents digital music shows and would have sex with a member of Razorlight in a wardrobe.
- A tuxedo with leather trousers. Terrible look. Usually adopted by a forty-something lothario recently divorced for banging his way round the local tennis club.
- Cowboy boots on a man. Women can get away with them, but it's only acceptable on a man if he's actually a cowboy.
- A blazer and shorts. Blazers are a problem at the best of times. Most people see someone in a blazer and think 'dick'. The fact that people still wear blazers is testament to the frightening fact that there are enough people out there for whom this isn't a problem, who are shielding blazer-wearers from the rest of us. But put a blazer together with shorts and you have a look that says 'Kick me, and don't stop till I'm on the outskirts of your town'.

If we focus in further, we can see how some garments are cool and uncool according to the chosen fabric. Take the waistcoat. Fine if worn with a suit. And without a jacket, a waistcoat can be cool if you're Russell Brand or are the editor of a frontier-town newspaper during the Yukon gold rush.

But wearing it on its own without a shirt is inexcusable unless you are the saxophone player in Tina Turner's band. And even then you've got to ask some serious questions about your life choices. Even worse than that is a leather waistcoat – listen up, pal, you're not in *The Matrix*, you work in Games Workshop and have a copy of *Dragonheart* hidden under your mattress. There's only one step further down and that's a leather waistcoat with your name written in studs on the back. There's simply no excuse for that outside of 'I am a fighter in the Thunderdome.'

Don't forget that there's nothing wrong with the classics – a well-cut suit, a pressed white shirt, hand-crafted leather shoes. For a casual look, think jeans. The thing about a truly classic look is that it can't be uncool. No one ever says 'I'm so over Miles Davis' or 'Steve McQueen's a bit passé'. These things are set in stone. The thing about cool is not to try too hard. If you start wearing a fireman's helmet, pin-striped jacket, long johns and cowboy boots, you will have created a unique look, and, yes, 'unique' is an essential part of cool. But it's contrived, and contrivance kills cool like the chancing upon yet another TV show with Peter and Jordan can kill your will to live.

It's cool to think of your favourite Beatle or Bond. But not your favourite Chuckle Brother

How to Have Cool Hair

People spend a lot of time and money on their hair; it's one of the first things you notice on a person, and is key to conveying coolness. But it can also convey uncoolness. You must resist the lure of the following styles:

- The bowl cut – it makes you look like a medieval peasant or member of The Inspiral Carpets, circa 1990.
- Short and gelled forward – normally goes with Ben Sherman shirts, white trainers and a night on the town that ends with a fight over a bus seat.
- The mullet – this has seen something of a comeback in recent years. It still looks ridiculous. And once you've had a mullet, even though you get rid of it, you are haunted by its ghost. Pat Sharp has haunted hair.
- The perm – don't get me wrong, it's hilarious. But you have to understand that the coolest man with a perm is Brian May. And he wears clogs.
- Dreadlocks on a white person – on a black person, dreadlocks look cool, a statement of cultural pride and identity. On a white person, it just looks like you don't wash.
- The comb-over – this is about as convincing as the vows at someone's fifth wedding. Everyone knows the truth, and just because they're not saying it out loud, it doesn't mean it goes away.

- Tom Hanks' hairstyle in *The Da Vinci Code* – never have a haircut that makes it look like you've gelled it with vegetable oil.

How to Have a Cool Walk

A walk is key: it flags up your coolness from a distance. Think it, then you'll move it, and others will feel it.

MEN
You don't just have to look cool, you have to move cool. Think of Sean Connery. When Bond producer Cubby Broccoli saw him walk down the street, he knew he'd found his Bond because the man moved like a panther. That means he was lithe and fluid, all muscle and sinew, not that he was climbing a tree with a stolen goat in his mouth. You've got to get that reaction. Think like your favourite movie star, but make sure it's from one of their finer moments, not from that stage of their career where they said to their agent 'I've just had a massive tax bill, so whatever it is, the answer's "yes"!'

John Travolta – go for the strut from *Saturday Night Fever*, not the fat-necked bloat of *Battlefield Earth*.

John Wayne – walk like a gunslinger, but pushed too far it can look like a drunk man with one testicle trapped outside the elasticated band of his underpants.

Tom Cruise – no one runs like the Cruiser. There's such conviction and dedication. Just don't follow it through to jumping on a sofa proclaiming love for someone half your age, or getting really angry about the history of psychiatry.

Al Pacino – he moves great in *Heat*, like a hunter circling his prey. He's all restless energy. He's even got a cool walk as a blind man in *Scent Of A Woman*. I'd avoid the walk from *Dog Day Afternoon*, though, which is the frenetic pace of a man holding up a bank to pay for his lover's sex change operation.

Cary Grant – now *he* looks cool. It's effortless ease and can't be faked. Debonair, suave, sophisticated, all of these things are in his walk. Imagine there's a queue where coolness is handed out. Well, everyone else waited in the wrong place and Cary Grant copped the lot. He's the inverse of Norman Tebbit.

WOMEN

A cool walk is difficult for women, because it's so much more understated than a man's stride. Don't try to emulate a catwalk model, they look weird and it'll just make people wish you'd fall over. Not too much arse-shaking and hair-tossing either, it's trying too hard. Basically, just try not to bump into things and you're ahead of the game. Remember that men are looking for excuses *not* to sleep with women, not excuses *to*, and 'not having a cool walk' isn't even on their list of possible negatives.

How to Have A Cool Accent

The thing about accents is that nobody thinks they have one. Within the British Isles, the coolest accents are Scottish and Irish. Hands down. Geordie's pretty cool, and Scouse has been re-evaluated. But all of these are blown out of the water by the French, Italians and Spanish: they could turn you on reading a ransom demand. The Germans still sound like they're about to summon fire and vengeance, the Russians like they're going to throw you from the roof of a car park. Despite their idiot president, most Americans still sound damn cool. But when Brits go over there, they all think we're Hugh Grant or Audrey Hepburn, so it works both ways.

How to Talk Cool

'Cowabunga!' 'Whassup!' 'Not!' 'Acieed!' The language of cool changes quicker than the ways most people would like to hurt the members of Westlife (a friend of mine can list 243 different pain-inflicting techniques, not even counting the ways he says he'd like to get Bryan McFadden to beg for mercy). It's fine, though, to adopt the sayings of the day; where it becomes uncool is in overuse. Of course modern British urban patois, or 'Blinglish', is very cool, deriving as it does from the speech patterns of American hip hop. But the danger is that this, too, will date, as has the language of the speakeasys and early jazz. So 'Yo bro, you feelin' me in da house?' may soon sound as archaic as 'Perch here, doll, I'll go and see which one of these cats has some suck with the maitre d'.

So go neutral with your speech: no fancy phrases that can date you or link you to a particular movement. And remember that, often, the less you say the cooler you are. It makes you seem mysterious, deep and alluring. Of course you might be thick as pig shit, but at first people will give you the benefit of the doubt.

COOL INSTRUMENTS
Guitar, piano, saxophone
UNCOOL INSTRUMENTS
Swanee whistle, paper and comb, hollowed out skull

How to Have a Cool Nickname

Everyone wants a nickname, right? Wrong. Everyone wants a *cool* nickname. Nicknames are a shorthand CV, an introduction to you and your worldview. Here are some nicknames you don't want:

- Tight Bastard
- Sperm Bank
- Stella Sweat
- Bin-Juice Drinker
- Tramp Fucker
- Uncle C**t
- Rapey John

Now we don't get to choose our nicknames. They usually arise out of a particular incident or mode of behaviour. They can be something that reflects a single out-of-character incident that your friends jokingly don't want you to forget. Or it can be something you're known for doing/saying on a regular basis. But you don't get to choose it. There's nothing more annoying than meeting someone who says 'My name's Jack, but everyone calls me "Creme Egg" because I once shoved five creme eggs up my arse.' You think, 'I'm probably not going to call you anything because I don't want you in my social circle. I might leave the room and return to find you naked with your balls tucked between your legs trying to

down a pint of crème de menthe whilst dancing to Billy Idol.'
You can't force a nickname, it has to flow out of you. So you
want a cool nickname? Act cool and it'll follow. You could be
known as

- 'GT', because you always drink gin and tonic. Well, not
  solely, although if you did you'd be the most
  sophisticated tramp in the park.
- 'LM', short for 'Ladies Man', because of your charm and
  ease with the fairer sex. Hopefully not because you
  consistently use the wrong toilets.
- 'CG' or 'Cary', because you look like Cary Grant. This is
  really cool. As long as you don't actually work as his
  lookalike.
- 'Babyface', because you look young. Not because you
  often need winding, or usually have food and/or vomit on
  your chin.
- 'Legend'. Cool nickname. For whatever reason, whether it's
  your stamina on the sports field, your capacity for drink
  or the fact you always come through for your friends
  when they need you. Not so cool if the name's derived
  from your love and obsession with the 1985 Ridley Scott
  fantasy film of the same name.
- 'The Hulk'. You're big and strong, or maybe have a
  temper. Hopefully not from your habit of waking up
  amongst the bins in ripped trousers with no memory of
  the night before.

- 'Captain Solo'. You look like Harrison Ford, or have the carefree rule-bending attitude of Han Solo. Or you are a proud proponent of the noble and ancient art of self-pleasure.
- 'Dirty Harry'. You look like Clint Eastwood and are good at bluffing – at Poker, say, as opposed to bluffing at the number of bullets left in your gun. That's cool. Not so cool if your moniker derives from an incident where you got so drunk you soiled yourself.

How to Have a Cool Tattoo

Twenty years ago, tattoos were the preserves of sailors and convicts. Now everyone has them. I'm not the only person to predict a sorry-looking generation on the beach in fifty years' time. Wrinkled and faded images, like a felt-tip essay left in the rain. When choosing a tattoo, be aware that it is purely decorative. Having the Chinese for 'warrior' written on your shoulder doesn't actually make you a warrior. Having your child's name tattooed on your back doesn't make you a better parent. If anything, it shows fiscal irresponsibility. That money would be better invested in some kind of trust fund to pay for their university fees, or to go towards a deposit on a flat. Cool tattoos tend to be things like:

- Celtic patterns
- Peace symbols
- Chinese dragons

Where it all goes wrong is when there's too many. People with blue arms and legs look weird. They look like Biker Smurfs. Some people also overdo it with long, flowing scripts and quotations. Angelina Jolie, for instance, seems to have got her lower abdomen confused with a notebook. Less is more if you want to look cool with a tattoo. Also avoid tattoos of the following:

- Your favourite porn star
- A list of people you've had sex with
- A list of people you'd like to have sex with
- Lightning bolts down your inner thigh
- The cast of *The Care Bears Movie*
- 'My other body's a titanium exoskeleton'
- 'Leonardo DiCaprio 4 Ever'
- 'I love Johnny Hates Jazz'

How to Have Cool Piercings

We're living in the future now! You can look like a warrior from a metal planet! And you can look cool! Unless you

- Get a piercing if you're over forty, it smacks of a 'crisis'
- Get addicted to it and tell everyone you're being converted into a cyborg
- Get a cock ring and then either a) bore people by going on and on about how it enhances your sexual performance OR b) revolt people by going on and on about the infection you picked up because the guy didn't sterilise his needle or hole punch or whatever the hell he used

THE LOOK COOLOMETER TEST

1 You are having a bad hair day. Do you

a) Buy a disposable razor and shave it off, claiming an infestation of 'space lice'

b) Say to everyone you meet 'I sat on a battery, whaddya know!'

c) Buy a hat or shrug it off

d) Say 'I had a fight with a lawnmower. You want to see the state of the lawnmower. I fucked it up real bad. That bitch ain't going to be mowing lawns for a while!'

2 You discover that your nickname at work is 'Tighty', because you never buy a round. Do you

a) Bring in bottles of wine you've laced with laxatives and afterwards gloat 'I'm tight and you're all loose, what feels better?'

b) Try to claim compensation on the grounds of monetarist discrimination

c) Make a mental note to buy rounds in future

d) Call a meeting where you explain that money's tight because you're saving up for your sister's kidney operation and then have a whip-round, which you spend on booze

3 **Somebody notices your favourite hat hanging up and unknowingly makes a joke about the kind of person who would wear such a garment. Do you**

a) Tear it into pieces which you force down their throat till you're hauled off by startled onlookers

b) Scream 'At least I don't dress like a sex offender!'

c) Pick it up and put it on

d) Start stripping whilst singing 'You Can Leave Your Hat On'

4 **Whilst walking through a town square or shopping precinct, you notice that everyone else is sitting down and all eyes are on you. Do you**

a) Sing 'I can see through your clothes with my special robot eyes! And your breasts and penises are lacking in size!'

b) Try and hide in a bin

c) Walk with rhythm and purpose

d) Walk like an Egyptian whilst singing the Bangles 'Manic Monday', then ask for any loose change people feel like donating for this feat of mental energy

5 You arrive at a party or event underdressed. Do you
a) Knock someone out and steal their clothes
b) Accuse the person who invited you of trying to make
   you look like an idiot by not telling you the dress code,
   and demand financial recompense for the damage
   done to your public image
c) Explain you had to rush there from work
d) Leave, yelling abuse at what you term 'Dress Code,
   Apartheid'

If you answered mainly 'a', not good. You dress like a
   shepherd and dance like a member of the Royal Family.
If you answered mainly 'b', you are Pete Burns.
If you answered mainly 'c', you can be seen in public,
   strut your stuff with confidence. Though not like John
   Travolta in *Saturday Night Fever*, he's a dick.
If you answered mainly 'd', you have no dress sense
   whatsoever and may possibly be a Labour MP from the
   seventies.

Chapter 4

HOW TO BE COOL . . .
AT WORK

How to be Cool at a Job Interview

Job interviews are like first dates: they involve a lot of positive image projection. Or to put it another way, lying. Here's what you feel like saying:

- 'Why do you want to come and work here?' *Money*
- 'What are your interests outside of work?' *Sex with multiple partners*
- 'What do you think you'll bring to the company?' *Genital warts*

Everyone knows you're saying what *they* want to hear, so how can you be cool in an environment where everyone's motives are exposed? In films, of course, the candidate who gets the job is the one who cuts the crap and tells it like it is. You know, feet up on the desk: 'Let's get this bullshit over, I know you're seeing hundreds of people for this toothless position in your craphole company, so don't waste my motherfuckin' time!' Cue interviewers going into a huddle. 'Well he/she certainly has attitude, what a breath of fresh air, we'd like to offer you the job', etc. Now while in reality this

77

ultra-cool approach cannot be guaranteed as successful, and may even backfire spectacularly with you being thrown out by security for lighting up in the waiting room, there are some elements to be woven into giving a cool job interview.

The important thing is not to act to keen. Obviously you want the job, but don't look too needy: you're hot right now and are getting plenty of offers. The subtle undercurrent should be that you're interviewing them. Of course this will only work for jobs of a certain status. You can't act all 'Well what am I going to get from this?' if you've answered an advert for fruit pickers, or for people to hand out free newspapers at the side of the road.

Body language is important. Look relaxed and confident. Somewhere between slouching with your legs open and looking like you're on parade with a particularly scary drill sergeant.

They say you should always mention a fault, as it shows honesty, but make it something that can seem like a positive. So not 'I'm a petty thief' or 'I like to stalk people. I'm following a few of your staff, and a job here will really make the day shifts easier'. One of these will do:

- 'I can't switch off till I've finished a task'
- 'I don't leave enough time for my personal life'
- 'My superior qualities will make my colleagues question the validity of every aspect of their existence'

Put all this together and not only will you come across as cool, you'll also get the job.

> There is nothing uncooler than wetting yourself on a fairground ride as an adult

How to be Cool on Your First Day at Work

First impressions count, and you have to convey different things to different people in a short space of time. To the management, you must convey that you are a vital new addition to their workforce who will go the extra mile for the company. To your fellow workers, you need to give the impression you are up for a laugh – you're the sort of person who might liven up a stuffy party by dancing on a piano. Basically, you've got to look like you don't take orders. But actually you have to take them or you'll be sacked.

So be polite and industrious when the management are looking, and offer to buy everyone in your team a drink after work. It may sound pricey, but it shows you are fun and generous; you'll be known as a cool person. Don't skimp here by handing out miniatures you've nicked from planes and encouraging people to neck them with you as they walk to their cars. And don't alienate your new colleagues by sucking up to management too much and saying things like 'I'm a good link, but there's a lot of slack in this chain'.

Also, don't ignore the subclass of cleaners and delivery-men. If you acknowledge them and you're a man, you look cool, because it shows there are no social barriers you aren't prepared to smash. Plus, they may turn a blind eye when at a later date you steal ink cartridges or put a portion of road-kill in the desk drawer of a colleague for reasons best known to yourself. Women talking to deliverymen etc., on the other hand, is always cool because of the frisson of flirting. It makes you feel cool that there's a dirty-handed man you could hump in the car park stairwell. And it's also a way of letting that guy in marketing you fancy know you're single and up for it. Don't lay it on too thick, though. Go with 'What's a single girl to do on Valentines?' rather than 'I'll be begging for it in the Yates's Wine Bar'.

Remember that the cardinal rule is not to try too hard to be cool on your first day. So, if you're a guy, don't go round in a makeshift bandana referring to the other men as 'homs' and the women as 'bitches'. And if you're a woman, don't think that being cool means looking through anyone who smiles at you or having a belt with a buckle that says 'Moschino' – what that really says is 'Slagweasel'.

How to be Cool in the Tea Break

Keep the chat light and amusing. Don't go for ultra-cool aloofness by sitting in a corner in mirrored shades chewing a matchstick and pursing your lips every time someone you fancy hoves into view. But equally don't be too everyday and bore people with your problems. No one really cares if you suspect your husband's extra squash games might be the cover for an affair. Or how annoying it is when your girlfriend's gay best friend comes in for tea after shopping with her and interrupts your viewing of *Doctor Who* with a stream of gay innuendo that, frankly, you do not see as a major subtext. And don't be too precious about your mug. As long as you've got something to drink out of, it doesn't really matter. If the use of your mug by another person annoys you to the point that you find yourself staying late to roll it round the floor of the toilet, then you probably need to take some time off.

How to be Cool in the Lunch Hour

There can be a real hierarchy at lunch hour. It's like at school – the cool kids can congregate together in a clique that excludes others. Here are some tips:

- If you're in a clique, you're not as cool as you think you are. If you're in one of those quiet cliques that stares and murmurs, intimidating others through stillness, then stop right now. You are no worse or better than the other people who work there. You may sneer at the people who get excited at the release of Rod Stewart's *Great American Songbook Volume 3*, but they are actually happy. Whereas you are the type of people who will talk about how disappointed you've been by Scorsese's recent efforts, or those of Kate Bush, despite never having done anything in your miserable fucking lives.

- If you are a loud, noisy clique that gives a little shriek or cheer whenever one of your number enter the room, then please take a moment to think about how twattish your forced jollity really is. Maybe it's time to focus on the things you try to shut out – like the roaring indifference of the cosmos to the very existence of mankind, let alone you, a tiny speck of its multitudinous detritus.

The most important thing to remember is never, ever, ever start a conga line. Whether it's a wacky proposal or a Red Nose Day prank, it reeks of wankdom.

How to be Cool at the Christmas Party

This is a really tricky one to get right. It has all the concerns of every tea and lunch break compressed into one horrendous evening. As ever, there's a balance between aloofness and trying too hard. Here are some handy dos and don'ts:

DO – Have a dance at some point in the evening. It shows that you don't take yourself too seriously.

DON'T – Dance like a robot, exotic dancer, astronaut on a space walk, or Wookie on heat.

DO – Exhibit platonic tactility. Hug people. Spread a little love.

DON'T – Wear one of those hats with mistletoe sticking out of the top. In terms of sexual creepiness, it's one up from night-vision goggles and a net.

DO – Give cards to the people you really like.

DON'T – Make a collage with pictures of you and them and the words 'Bestest Buddies' written in pasta shells underneath.

DO – Sing along to *Now That's What I Call Christmas*.

DON'T – Bring in a portable keyboard, distribute carol sheets and threaten to punch anyone who doesn't join in with your bossa nova version of 'Once In Royal David's City'.

DO – Make a play for that person you've been flirting with for several months.

DON'T – Get drunk and cling to their leg crying 'Just hold me! I'm so alone! It's like living in a prison of fucking ice!'

How to be Cool When You've Been Caught Downloading Pornography

Now this depends on the evidence against you. If someone in IT has traced downloads from an adult site to your password protected PC, you can maybe blame an error in the system, or say that someone else has been doing it. Whether this works will depend on your image around the office. It will be easier if you are a clean-cut man in a stable relationship, or a woman, as people will be less ready to believe you look at pornography in the first place. Trickier to protest your innocence if you are a male known for lewd and inappropriate remarks, or go to strip clubs in your lunch hour.

If you were caught in flagrante, i.e. pants down, then you have a number of options to save face, but few will clinch you any cool points, you're too far down the track. But here goes:

- Claim the other person is hallucinating. They're the real sex pest!

- You're carrying out a personal assignment from the highest authority on a need-to-know basis and any mention of this encounter will result in instant dismissal.
- You were doing a full system check for medical reasons.
- 'I'll stop what I'm doing right now if you promise not to tell anyone!'
- 'I'll finish off what I'm doing right now if you promise not to tell anyone!' (NB This is an extremely high-risk strategy and can result in the other party making demands upon you that you may not feel comfortable fulfilling.)

How to be Cool When You Have the Most Hated Job in the Office

This could be any number of positions. You could have one of those nebulous job titles that seem to describe a completely extraneous position, such as 'Assistant Vice-President Executive Brand Manager'. You could be one of those bosses who do nothing except flounce in, make stupid suggestions, forget you insisted on a course of action, then try to fire people who followed your diktats. You could be in Human Resources, which to me still sounds like the name of some hideous corporation in a David Cronenberg film that provides cloned body parts, or homeless people for manhunts. Whatever your position, the given is that no one likes you or respects you. How do you maintain your cool in the face of such an undercurrent of hostility? The key is not to come out guns blazing. It's not going to help if you start snarling things like 'I don't give a rat's arse what you drongos think of me. I look at my pay packet and you just melt away!' Cool is about detachment. It's best to kill them with kindness. Bring in chocolates and wine on the last Friday of every month. Buy tickets for bands you've no intention of seeing then offer the tickets round for free on a group email because 'your partner's parents have just come to stay'. Turn a blind eye to people calling in sick on the day of major sporting fixtures. Basically, you have to bribe the affections of your colleagues and underlings.

How to be Cool when You Fancy Someone New But You Have the Reputation in the Workplace of Being, Shall We Say, Somewhat Loose

I'm prepared to believe that your looseness could be the result of circumstantial evidence. You may have had several dates too many that never went anywhere, maybe a few short-term non-starter relationships. You might just be one of those people who know when a relationship isn't going to go anywhere so you stop it early on. Or, let's face it, you could just be a bit of a slag. Of the male or female variety. Whatever the source or cause of the rumours, you can't try and pre-empt them, it'll look like you're protesting too much. But they will hear them, and it may make them back off. No one likes to feel like they're a name on a list of conquests, it's just not that cool. OK, all those women who sleep with Russell Brand and Colin Farrell might find it cool to be on their lists. But if a guy's famous, women change the rules – all that 'I hardly know you' crap goes straight out of the window. And whilst most men don't mind some stranger grabbing them in a bar or club, they don't want to see them every day at work. Especially not if they lowered their standards out of sheer desperation, or simply because it was on offer. So, if you want this person, but you've been around the office like crabs on a cruise ship, you need a new approach. Your best course of action is to make a subtle play for them, and when they respond, act like they're coming on too strong, it's all a bit quick. This will put them on the back foot. When they then imply you have the reputation of putting out at the drop of a hat, you can explain that's a vicious rumour put about by an ex, or someone whose feelings you hurt when you turned them down. This will make you look mature and sensitive, all of which whack up your cool quotient. (NB if you do end up sleeping with them but don't want it to be a long term thing, don't think it's quicker, easier or cooler to get rid of them by saying 'Oh, all that stuff about me is true. I go through partners like locusts in a field of wheat.' There are plenty of cool excuses in the 'How To Be Cool When Dumping People' section, and as you'll discover, honesty is never the way!)

> **COOL THINGS TO BE A CHAMPION AT**
> Surfing, boxing, driving, running
> **UNCOOL THINGS TO BE A CHAMPION AT**
> Sheep-shearing, hotdog eating, the Rubik's Cube

How to be Cool When Given a Promotion

Really cool people also have grace, so, when given a promotion, don't jump all over the desks of your colleagues, with your coat around your shoulders as a cape, pointing alternately at your arse and their face whilst 'Simply The Best' plays tinnily from your iPod headphones. Play it down. But not to the point of 'It's the least I deserve, I'm wasted on these donkeys'. If someone congratulates you, turn the focus of the conversation onto them and their achievements and potential.

How to be Cool When Passed Over for a Promotion

Just as coolness requires composure in the face of good fortune, you must also keep your dignity when misfortune comes a calling. Say you've been overlooked for a promotion in favour of a colleague you feel is less qualified for the position than you. The reasons for this unfairness play over and over in your mind. Maybe the dice just rolled against you this time? Maybe they socialise more with the upper echelons of management? Maybe they kidnapped a loved one and blackmailed your boss? Whatever the reason, take it on the chin. Just walk up to them in full view of your colleagues, shake hands, look them in the eye, and say 'Congratulations, you really deserve this.' No matter how tempting it is to launch a whispering campaign against them, do not stoop to it. Nor should you stay late and place a small quantity of dog shit inside their mouse. (Your plan is that, before they find it, the stench will have got into their mouse mat, desk and on to their hand, and so people will start saying things like 'They're all right, but their hand smells of dog shit' and you will enjoy a quiet and unacknowledged victory.) But it is bad karma and it will eat away at you.

How to be Cool at Your Leaving Do

The cool way to behave at your leaving do depends on the circumstances surrounding your departure. For instance, if you are in your twenties and have been headhunted for a better position and more money by a rival firm, then that's pretty cool on it's own. You don't need to dress that up. Just work the room and be gracious. If, however, you are in your twenties and have been asked to leave a) because you're useless and/or b) because you gave them a reason to sack you when you put a Tampax in the toaster, then there's not really much of 'cool' spin that can be applied.

COOL REASON TO BE LEAVING A JOB – You've won the lottery and want to travel

UNCOOL REASON TO BE LEAVING A JOB – You reckon that, after tax and National Insurance, you'll make just as much on benefits

COOL REASON TO BE LEAVING A JOB – Pregnancy/to be a house husband

UNCOOL REASON TO BE LEAVING A JOB – Working hours are getting in the way of your 'Wanking Schedule'

COOL REASON TO BE LEAVING A JOB – A philanthropic billionaire wants you to manage a scheme to provide clean drinking water in the Indian subcontinent

UNCOOL REASON TO BE LEAVING A JOB – You did a wee in the water cooler

COOL REASON TO BE LEAVING A JOB – You've been recruited by MI6

UNCOOL REASON TO BE LEAVING A JOB – You were caught fitting cameras in opposite gender's toilets

COOL REASON TO BE LEAVING A JOB – You've reached retirement age after lifetime of quiet and respected dedication

UNCOOL REASON TO BE LEAVING A JOB – You've reached retirement age after lifetime of vicious backstabbing, racial slurs and out of court settlements concerning sexual harassment on conference weekends

WORK COOLOMETER TEST

1 Your boss tells you off for being repeatedly late. Do you

a) Smash all the clocks in the building screaming 'We must defeat the Time Nazis!'

b) Say 'Suck a fat one, clockwatcher! Miles Davis never kept time on stage or at the bar!'

c) Apologise and explain you'll make up the time by working later

d) Say 'Sure, I'll just make love four times a night instead of five!'

2 It's the Christmas Party, a drunk colleague you don't fancy wants to take you home. Do you

a) Ask for money up front and insist you both wear protective suits

b) Silence the party, tell everyone what they said, and then mime throwing up in a bucket

c) Politely decline and put them in a taxi home

d) Laugh in their face and moonwalk off backwards to the centre of the room, blowing kisses as you do

3 **It's your first day and you don't know where the toilet is. Do you**

a) Go in a bag and throw it out of the window

b) Ask where the toilet is, then drag someone in to show you exactly how 'the apparatus' works

c) Ask where the toilet is

d) Clap your hands and rap 'Hey you, show me to the loo! I'm new, unlike you, and I need a poo!'

4 **It's your last day. Do you**

a) Try to dig a tunnel out of the building, claiming you've learnt the lessons of *The Shawshank Redemption*

b) Barricade yourself in a cupboard with food, water and a flashlight

c) Ask people to join you for farewell drinks in a nearby bar

d) March through the office dressed like Keanu Reeves in *The Matrix* to Rainbow's 'Since You Been Gone'

5 **You find yourself in a room with someone you've nodded at for years but never actually spoken to. Do you**

a) Fall to the floor screaming 'I've seen you in my dreams, you've come to take my soul!'
b) Listen to your iPod with your eyes shut, opening them occasionally and giggling when you catch sight of them
c) Introduce yourself, apologising that it's taken this long
d) Say 'You should get a photo of us together, because I add muchos kudos to your socialos standingos'

If you answered mainly 'a', your colleagues would rather be homeless than spend another day looking at your stupid face.

If you answered mainly 'b', not good – I'd check under your car before you start the engine.

If you answered mainly 'c', you are popular, like Tony Blair in 1997. Try not to start an unjustified war.

If you answered mainly 'd', you think you are a beloved office joker, but will die a lonely and unmourned death and rot in an unvisited grave.

Chapter 5
HOW TO BE COOL . . . SOCIALLY

Social gatherings are battlegrounds of cool, with everyone scrambling to come out on top. Every advert, every film, every music video tells us we have to be elegant beings of poise who never do or say the wrong thing. Yet most of us have on occasion walked into a party and felt like Worzel Gummidge trying to join the Rat Pack. This section will aim to lessen those moments, and make people say 'I want to know them' when you walk into a room rather than 'They could help protect my crops.'

How to be Cool in a Bar

If it's a regular haunt, it's nice to have your own signature drink. It's a way of branding yourself as cool. People know you're consistent. Here's a quick guide to the types of cool that different drinks confer:

- Gin and tonic – cool and stylish. The drink of a lawyer kicking back after a hard day's shuffling paper.
- Belgian beer – a person of taste and distinction. You like an elevated version of a common drink. You're the sort of

person who might have a season ticket for a football team, but it was probably a gift from a client and you don't get to all the matches.

- Two pints of lager and three double vodka tonic chasers – you are a chronic alcoholic and probably live in a skip.
- Vodka and Red Bull – you are a woman of easy virtue.
- Guinness – not too imaginative, but it's solidly soulful. Just don't make any cracks about black stools as you down it.
- Milk – you are a weirdo.
- Tequila Slammers – you would probably down a pint of your own piss for a packet of peanuts.
- (NB do not choose Malibu and pineapple juice as your signature drink. It's drunk exclusively by arseholes.)

There are also ways of behaving in a bar that convey different levels of coolness.

IF YOU'RE ON YOUR OWN

Look charismatic and independent. You want people to feel they should come and talk to you, but at the same time that you're quite happy on your own. Don't lay it on too thick – no laughing at your own brilliant thoughts, no look of wide-eyed horror as though you're a detective who's just realized his own Chief of Police is the killer. You've got to look like you don't care that people might know you're there on your own.

IF YOU'RE IN A GROUP

Don't be too loud, as that's just irritating. You should draw attention to yourself through your understated behaviour. It's a hard thing to get right. Look too detached and you risk coming across as someone who thinks they're better than everyone else in the room, which, if you're in a Wetherspoon's or Harvester, you probably are.

How to be Cool on the Dancefloor

This is a tricky one. Unless you're an amazing dancer, e.g. Michael Jackson before 'all that', don't even bother. You have to be good enough so that everyone forms a circle around you clapping in time and cheering at particular moves. Otherwise, just stand at the side nodding sagely.

It is extremely uncool to have a tiger's head mounted on your wall or on the back of your jacket

How to be Cool at a Club

Your first instinct, in order to look cool at a club, might be to pop on some dark glasses. Uh-oh. It's a little bit 80s. A little bit soap star on the slide. And it's a little bit 'stalky'. That's a basic rule, but for further advice, your behaviour and level of coolness must fit the type of club you're at.

PRIVATE MEMBERS CLUB

Don't stare at anyone famous. The cool thing to do is clock them but act like you're used to moving in those circles. You're not disrespecting them, you're just giving them space. And that doesn't come across if you stagger up to them singing one of their songs/theme tune from their TV show/ quoting lines from one of their films. Especially if you get the wrong song or quote. A friend of mine once ran up to Sting singing 'Nikita' by Elton John. He then asked for an auto-graph, which Sting understandably denied because he'd sung someone else's song. My friend then proceeded to argue with Sting that it was, in fact, his song. As though he might have forgotten his own back catalogue. Just typing this now makes me want to dig a hole and bury myself, and I wasn't even there. The other thing to remember is that, in these types of clubs, the drinks are priced so high you could be forgiven for saying 'I asked for a gin and tonic, not a nuclear secret' when presented with the bill. Again, though, the cool thing is to pay without breaking a sweat. You also have to dress well. Although, sometimes at these places the cool 'look' is all over the place style-wise. Suits are cool – designer, not off the peg BHS. But so are jeans, trainers and a faded T-shirt with a logo for a Mexican carwash. It's very hard to predict, all normal cool bets are off. The one thing I would say is, if you're a man, don't wear those three-quarter length trousers, and if you're a woman, don't go with culottes. In both cases they're ever so French. Now, don't get me wrong, the French are one of the coolest races on the planet. But it's a little bit *too* French. You can have too much of a cool thing. It's one step away from mime and pretending not to understand English.

TOP NIGHTCLUB

Well, for a start, you have to be on the guest list. There's no point standing in line in the cold – cool people do not have time to queue. This club needs you to give it cred. It needs you more than you need it. That's a load of crap, obviously, but you need to get into that mindset. And how satisfying is it to get a bizarre handshake greeting off a bouncer, to have the rope held back for you as you sashay past all the cattle in the queue staring at you with hate and envy! Once inside, there are various rules of behaviour that must be adhered to for coolness to emanate. Now, if you're like me, you're now at an age where it feels right to say things like 'The music is so loud in those places! You can't talk to anyone! You end up shouting and giving yourself a sore throat!' But you're in there trying to look cool. You can't pull out earplugs and a good book. Just nod and smile at people. You're not there to talk anyway. You're there to be seen. So be visible, but not in a needy way. Dress so people will assume you're someone of importance. But not literally, e.g. surgeon's gown or aqua-lung. You have to *command* attention without looking like you're *demanding* it. This is tricky and confusing. It's like a Zen thing. Chase it, and it goes. Just don't dance on the bar in leather trousers or ask the DJ for anything by Katie Melua and you'll be all right.

MIDDLING NIGHTCLUB

Go to the toilets of this club. Look above the urinal. Is there a poster advertising the 'Lovin' It Large Weekend Special! Guest DJ – Calum Best'? Yes? Then you're in a middling nightclub. There's no one of any real sophistication here. You'd think it would be easy to look cool in a place like this. Well, it is and it isn't. You can dress cool and act cool, but be prepared to hear things like 'Who the fuck do they think they are?' in passing. Show up in nice clothes asking for drinks they've never heard of, or send your G&T back because they've used the wrong brand of gin, and you can expect the natives to get very restless indeed. Meet them halfway. Dress down, drink lager, grab the arse of someone you fancy. Just don't sink to the lowest depths of hell, which is sitting on the dance floor pretending to row a boat to 'Oops Upside Your Head'.

DIRE NIGHTCLUB

The way to spot one of these is simple. Is it hard to tell the difference between the queue for the ladies and the queue for the gents? Can you smell vomit in the cloakroom? Have you walked through a metal detector? Do you suspect that the bouncers might plant a knife on you just for the fun of taking it off you? Are there no seats on the toilets? Has someone drawn a woman spreading her legs on the toilet door and burnt a section with their lighter to indicate the vagina? Are they playing Shania Twain's 'Man, I Feel Like A Woman' and are people dancing? If the answer to one or more of these questions is 'yes', then you are in a dire nightclub. You can look cool here by walking upright, but you risk scurvy, flogging and being boarded by pirates. All right, those are actually risks attached to being an eighteenth-century naval man, but they are more pleasant than the fate that may befall you in such a den of pissy bastards and shitty bitches.

How to be Cool at a Party Where You Don't Know Anyone

We've all been there. Invited by a friend who doesn't turn up, or a friend of a friend who vaguely recognises you but is too embarrassed or busy to introduce you to anyone else. So what do you do? Keep still and hope no one spots you? It's not much of an option. You might feel like you want the ground to swallow you up, or that you should literally pretend you're part of the furniture – crouching on all fours like a table or pretending to be a coat stand, but don't sink that low. There are other options. You can pretend to be texting someone. That'll take up about two minutes. If you calculate how often people look at you, you might be able to time it so that they think you're always texting. If you can't be bothered with that level of subterfuge and planning, you can ensure a night of texting by simply sending the message 'I'm not wearing any panties' to everyone in your phone's address book and then dealing with the replies. But you'll still look lonely and isolated. You could wander from room to room with drinks in your hand and a puzzled expression on your face as though you're looking for someone. But, again, that's a short-term solution and draws attention to your plight as people start to say to each other 'That person's been wandering round for an hour, I think they're pretending to look for someone.' No, if all you plan to do is fake texting and pretending you're lost, you may as well go home. The really cool person takes the plunge and walks up to a stranger, or group of strangers, introduces themselves, and lets the magic begin. You want them to leave going 'Who was that? What grace! What humour! What beauty! Did you see the way they moved!' Now that's a tall order for most of us, so here are some things to give you a head start:

IF YOU'RE A MAN APPROACHING A WOMAN

Make her feel like she's the most important person in the room. And ask questions. Show an interest in her mind, not just her body. Especially if she's below your normal par, you don't want to encourage someone and bed them out of pity.

IF YOU'RE A WOMAN APPROACHING A MAN

If you just want to get him into bed, dispense with all that laughing at his jokes and touching his arm stuff. Just say 'Would you like to go to bed?' It saves a lot of time and needless anecdotes. If you're using him to pinball to someone higher up the looks ladder, then by all means laugh at his jokes whilst making occasional eye contact with the stud muffin in the corner.

IF YOU'RE A MAN APPROACHING A GROUP OF WOMEN

OK, they know you've come over to do the chatting up equivalent of throwing shit at a wall. So just be yourself. Ask neutral questions about what they do, why they're there, who they know, etc. Charm = cool. Compliment them on their dress sense, or even better, their perfume. Don't go wacky and walk up with a bin on your head, or twirling a cocktail umbrella in your mouth: you'll look like a dick. If you want to wrong foot them, and get massive cool points, ask them for a female perspective on a dating problem, relationship issue, or what to do with your six-year-old niece when she comes to stay. It all says 'I'm comfortable with who I am, I don't mind appearing sensitive and vulnerable, and I'm a decent guy.'

IF YOU'RE A WOMAN APPROACHING A GROUP OF MEN

Be very wary, they will all assume you want to have sex with them, individually or as a group.

IF YOU'RE A MAN APPROACHING A GROUP OF MEN

Men don't really like other men who are cool. They feel intimidated and jealous and will insinuate that the cool man is probably a homosexual or a rapist. So play it low status, is my advice, then let your coolness seep out gradually.

IF YOU'RE A WOMAN APPROACHING A GROUP OF WOMEN

This is a bloody minefield. God knows what pecking order they've got set up, or who's got their eye on who. Play it all grateful and innocent and they'll take you under your wing. Best way in – tell them a sob story about a recent and painful break-up with a cheating boyfriend. They'll all rally round and you're in. And make sure you get the better of him in the end: you want to be cool and sassy, not a whining victim. Something to unite the sisterhood – nail varnish on his sports car or sour milk in the pockets of his suits. Don't get carried away and confess to an imaginary mock execution, or a paid-for assassination you don't know how to call off, though. Keep it within the realms of possibility and the law.

IF YOU'RE A MAN APPROACHING A MIXED GROUP

You've got to make the men want to be like you and the women want to sleep with you. How to take care of the men? Get them all drinks – easy. How to take care of the women? As before, talk to them like you don't want to sleep with them and you'll seem cool and unpredatory. And if you want a nutter, tell them you're married with kids. Nutters love it complicated and challenging.

IF YOU'RE A WOMAN APPROACHING A MIXED GROUP

Talk to the uncoolest-looking man in the group. It'll make his evening, and it'll pique the interest of the Richard Gere lookalike you really want. Or the Richard Madeley or Richard Whiteley lookalike, depending on your age and preferences.

> An eyepatch is cooler than a monocle

How to be Cool At Your Own Party

Hosting a party is very stressful. It's rather hard not to take it as a popularity indicator. But if the numbers are disappointing, don't let it show. Don't

- Get drunk in a corner and mouth off about how you might as well be dead
- Shut yourself in your room and watch DVDs with your headphones on
- Leave
- Text everyone who hasn't shown informing them you hope they get a painful kidney disease

Keep it loose and fun, be nice to the people who have turned up. Whatever you do, remember that it's not cool to

- Issue name badges
- Insist on playing games
- Charge people from their third drink onwards
- Silence people and read from your novel
- Get out a guitar and perform your song cycle based on the Apollo space missions

How to be Cool When Talking to Teenagers

When you're in your twenties, you want teenagers to think you're cool. This is because our culture values them as barometers of cool. Advertisers are obsessed with teenagers, they're the prime market, what they like rules. As you get older, it's tempting to want to gain their approval, to show that you've still got it, that you're still cool yourself. Then you move into your thirties and realise you don't give a damn what they think of you, they're all idiots! But if you want to seem cool to them, here's how to go about it:

- Stand your ground. Don't panic if there's an awkward pause and say things like 'So, what hot bands are around at the moment?' Make them ask you stuff: you're older, you've got more to say.
- Don't attempt to mimic their speech patterns with words like 'wicked', 'rad', 'bodacious' and 'bitching'. You'll be hopelessly out of date and out of your depth.
- Don't try to gain cool points with them by offering to buy them drink, drugs or fireworks.
- Don't try lowering the waistband of your trousers to reveal the top of your underpants. That sends a whole other signal that can get you on some sort of 'watch list'.

Just talk to them as you would anyone. The really cool person approaches all people as equals. Talk to them like they're adults, and they'll behave like adults. Although that's the sort of theory spouted by someone who's never had to deal with teenagers on a daily basis. Give them a week looking after one and they'll be marching on the streets waving placards demanding a return to National Service and the implementation of a curfew.

How to be Cool on Coming Into a Lot of Money

The temptation might be to buy a big gold sign saying 'Fuck You!' and drive it past the houses of everyone who's ever annoyed you. No. The cool thing to do is not to display conspicuous wealth. This is for two reasons:

1 It's ungracious and crass
2 People will know you're loaded and try and tap you for gifts and loans

It's also much more impressive when you meet someone, hit it off and go on a date, and your wealth comes as a surprise. Don't make a big thing of it as you walk them to your Porsche and whisk them off to your penthouse apartment. It's so much cooler than saying things like 'That's my

Porsche, it cost fifty thousand pounds. I paid cash!' or 'This flat is probably worth more than your lifetime income. Feel small?'

When it comes to clothes and décor, the thing to ask yourself is this – 'Would an international footballer buy this?' If the answer is yes, turn on your heel and walk out of the shop. It's much cooler to live modestly and give money to charity. Or at least pretend you do. In fact, you can give a pound a month to Oxfam and still say, with some degree of legitimacy, 'I give a proportion of my money to charity.' The way you came into money also affects how cool your fortune is. For instance

- Lottery win: not particularly cool, as it comes down to luck. Everyone around you will think 'That could have been me!' And they're right. Plus, if you're like most of the winners, you'll blow it on hiring nightclubs and building your own recording studio.
- Inheritance: if it's from your great aunt who you always got on with and tended in her final days, oblivious to her wealth, then that's pretty damn cool. From your estranged parents who unsuccessfully tried to cut you out of their will because you killed the family dog in a jealous rage, it's not so cool.

Of course you may have come into money because of some successful endeavour of your own undertaking. Again, the following are ultra-cool reasons for sudden colossal wealth that no one will have a problem with:

- Designer of wind farms
- Talented musician
- Actor with range and ability
- Footballer in skilful and admired tournament–winning team

Not so true for the following:

- Inventor of the plastic landmine which impedes shrapnel detection in wounds
- Member of boy or girl band
- Soap star
- Preening idiot regularly facing charges of sexual assault

Now a caveat: conspicuous wealth also depends on the tone of the purchase. Say you pay for a swimming pool. Fine. Have it in the shape of a guitar or a busty woman? Not fine. Flash car – cool. Personalised numberplate – generally not cool. Whatever it is, people tend to read it as 'I AM A NOB1'.

No one has ever looked cool wearing just one glove

How to be Cool as a Megastar

This is a really hard one to pull off. Spread your money around, you look like a show off. Don't spend it, you look like a miser. Give money to charity, everyone thinks you're doing it for the publicity. Give money to charity in secret, no one knows about it. Do your friends a favour by employing them in various capacities in your retinue, you've got yourself a posse, which makes you look like you need to pay people to suck up to you. Cool people are self-sufficient. They don't need people sucking up to them. Sure, a tight crew or a gang are cool. But not if they're money-grabbing freeloaders. Someone with a posse clearly has too much money. Likewise:

- Don't have your own airport like John Travolta. In this eco-sensitive age, that really is like chucking condoms at the Pope.
- Don't make diva-like demands. You don't need your dressing room repainted, or puppies in your rider. Just do your job and be grateful you get paid so much for what comes so easily.
- Don't moan about the pressure. Pressure is meeting the rent, paying food bills. You make enough to never worry about the essentials again, so don't get caught up in the peripheries, like what brand of scented candle Angelina Jolie has and how you have to have the same.

- Don't launch your own range of perfume, aftershave or clothing. We all know that means you go to a meeting, look at five samples, say 'that one', and take home a cheque for several million pounds. Singing and/or acting do not have skills that are transferable to perfumery or fashion. Ever hear of a perfumier releasing an album? No. Now piss off and do some work.

- You can adopt a child from another country. But don't use it to get on the front of magazines and then moan about press intrusion when you invited them to the orphanage.

DO NOT, UNDER ANY CIRCUMSTANCES, MAKE A SEX TAPE. How many more witless fools are going to document their sordid and inept couplings only to express surprise and regret when it's leaked on to the net? Surely they've cottoned on by now? If a man has a copy of that tape, he's going to show it to his friends. I'm not defending him, it's a despicable thing to do, but why else do you think he wants it filmed? For his personal records? To watch with you? No. He wants it to boast with. And surprise, surprise, you split up, like every couple in show business except Paul Newman and Joanne Woodward, and as an act of revenge and/or money-spinning, he or his friends put it out there. And you look about as cool as a farmer at the Oscars.

How to be Cool
When You're Teetotal

Just as there's nothing uncooler than a raging alcoholic, so it's true to say you don't want to go round looking like you've got a pole up your arse. If you're going to abstain, the key thing to get across is that you're not judging anyone who is. The coolest way of not drinking is to imply you've given up because you once had a real problem. There's no one wiser or cooler than a reformed alcoholic. Apart from a reformed heroin addict. They seem to be the coolest. It doesn't seem to work for other criminal acts or lapses in judgement. You can't get a round of applause on a chat show for saying 'I used to be a drink driver, but I haven't mown down a pedestrian in three years now!'

SOCIAL COOLOMETER TEST

1 You're in a nightclub when *Celebrity Love Island*'s Fran Cosgrave walks through the door. Do you

a) Insist on buying him a drink but cry when you discover they don't serve Ribena

b) Ask him for a quote for the Patrick Kielty biography you're writing

c) Leave

d) Ask him to describe in detail Jodie Marsh's genitalia

2 A friend's teenage son asks what music you're into. Do you

a) Pull out your iPod and rub it over your crotch saying 'Sex music!'

b) Say 'All kinds of stuff. You heard any Harold MacMillan and the Bluenotes? No, before your time. Not all stuff back from old 20C was thumbs down'

c) Give an honest reply

d) Say 'Pistols and The Clash, everything else is a lie. Although I do like jazzical – that's a mix of classical and jazz'

3 **A friend tells you they think you've had enough to
drink. Do you**

a) Freeze like a human statue and ignore them till they
walk away

b) Say 'You'll know when I've had enough. It's when I tell
you to fuck off. Now fuck off'

c) Thank them for their honesty and call for a taxi

d) Say 'Why you gotta clip my wings, dog? I'm living for
me, you and all the other squares out there who don't
got the balls to see the world as it is – one fucked up
ball of hope and despair'

4 **You find yourself alone at a party. Do you**

a) Take off a shoe, scream 'Mouse!' and crawl round on all
fours beating areas of the floor

b) Shout 'I feel lucky, anyone got any Johnnies?'

c) Engage a friendly-looking stranger in conversation

d) Go to the bathroom, draw a picture of Mick Jagger on
your chest in biro, then strip in the living room singing
'Please allow me to introduce myself! I'm [insert your
name]'

5 You have a little bit of a windfall from the Grand National. Do you

a) Go to a bar and lay out a trail of pound coins leading to your crotch

b) Start living on the streets to throw 'those grasping little bastards' off the scent

c) Throw a party for your friends

d) Buy a tailored white leather jumpsuit with the words 'Horny Moneyfucker' emblazoned in studs on the back

If you answered mainly 'a', it's bad: local pubs and clubs have lookouts warning of your arrival.

If you answered mainly 'b', maybe it's not a coincidence that whenever someone gives you a phone number, there's a digit missing.

If you answered mainly 'c', pretty good, you have a reputation as an affable well-liked person. Until someone sees what's in that box under your bed.

If you answered mainly 'd', people have jumped out of windows to avoid talking to you.

Chapter 6

HOW TO BE COOL . . .
IN THE URBAN
ENVIRONMENT

The modern city is a playground of cool. But beware, some of the swings are unsafe, and there may be rough boys from the estate who'll throw gravel on the base of the slide as you start your descent.

How to be Cool at the Gym

Gyms are cool, and certainly having a lithe and toned body is cool. As long as you're not obsessed by it. Don't go round getting people to feel your biceps or punch you in the stomach. But taking care of your physique and health is not to be sniffed at. Vanity is uncool, though, so don't start doing weights while looking in the mirror and saying things like 'Ooh, that's right! You looking good, bitch!' or 'Dang, I'm hot! Touch me, ouch!' Stay in shape, but pretend that it's no big deal; you don't make a special effort to keep trim, it's a natural part of your routine.

There is an art to looking cool while you're at the gym. But it's tricky, there's a lot of complicated machinery and the very real risk of producing noxious body odours. So go in looking like you know what you're doing. If you're new, try to book an induction when the gym is at it's emptiest, or when it's full of people you don't care about, i.e. Friday evening – what kind of person goes then? The kind of person who has no social life or whose partner is 'working late' again (clearly having an affair), that's who. It's imperative that, whenever anyone looks at you, you come across as someone who has been doing this for years as part of a regular fitness pro-gramme. I don't mean in terms of physique, you can't fake that if you're new to it and you are a bit on the hefty side. I'm talking about attitude. When you walk up to a machine, don't pull a face, look around for help, and then slope off. Just pull some levers, adjust the seat and do stuff. If you've started with too heavy a weight, for God's sake, don't stop and reduce it. Do the most you can, then walk away rolling your shoulders as if to say 'Yeah, one of those is enough for my programme. I'm developing specific muscle groups using a process of intense targeting.' And try not to look like you're about to collapse at any moment, no one wants to imagine a sexual partner who's going to say 'Stop, stop, my back!' or 'Ease up, I'm going to burst a blood vessel!' If you're not averse to cheating your cool points, you can always put the weight up to something ridiculous when you finish, so that the next person to use it will think 'Bloody hell, it's Hercules!' But if you're spotted doing that, your cool points go through the floor, as fraud is not cool.

Don't worry about sweating, it shows exertion, it shows commitment: you're pushing yourself to the limit. Having said that, there is a limit to the amount of sexiness that sweating can convey. A bib of sweat on a jogging man is fine. A sheen of sweat on a woman working her biceps is subtly arousing. A man looking like he's burst or just been chased across moorland by an escaped convict, less so.

Dress is also important at the gym. It's tempting to think 'I'm going to sweat and roll around on a mat, it doesn't matter what I wear!' It does if you want to look cool, and that's not going to work if you're in a Shed Seven tour T-shirt and school gym shoes. Dress stylishly. I mean gym stylish – same rules as normal dress, i.e. simple and classic. And above all, don't fall off the running machine. That's unrecoverable. That'll be replayed by the staff on CCTV. Basically, if that happens, you have to join another gym.

> Never be first on at a dance or an orgy

How to be Cool Driving a Car

For most of us, the driving experience consists of a lot of sitting and swearing as we edge forward in ten-yard spurts through anonymous urban sprawl. No amount of games – 'Count The Weeds', 'Crisp Packet Balloon Race', 'Ugly Man In Nice Car' – can relieve the tedium. You may even reach the point where branding yourself with the cigarette lighter seems like a fun idea.

But this dystopia is a fairly recent development. Driving and cars used to be cool. OK, some cars were always cooler than others – Ferraris, Porsches, Lamborghinis, etc. But nowadays it's an eco-political minefield. For some reason we've all decided that people who drive 4x4s in towns are the primary reason for global warming. Forget America producing 30 per cent of the world's greenhouse gases and the massive industrialisation programmes undertaken by India and China, the latter of which are intent on building hundreds of coal-fired power stations, not to mention the huge expansion in air travel. No, it's all the fault of that posh woman in Chelsea, and if we have a go at her, the whole problem will just go away. Right now a 'gas guzzling' 4x4 is the uncoolest car to drive. People will literally spit at you for driving it. So which cars can you drive and still be cool?

Well, you could get a Prius. They're a bit style-less, but they *are* eco-friendly. You could get a piddling little electric car, but they're one up from a golf cart. Though they will get you cool points in an 'I care about the planet' kind of way. Or you could always go the middle way and get a cool-looking car that isn't targeted as a planet killer. The new Audi TT is cool. It's basically a penis on wheels. It's impossible not to be cool in that. I'm talking, of course, as though money is no object here and conveniently forgetting that cars are incredibly expensive. That's why, even though the nice expensive ones are cool in a brochure and a showroom, it's a different story on the road. But that's the trade off with expensive cars generally. You may think you look cool in your Porsche, but everyone else looking at you, out of pure unhidden jealousy, thinks you're an absolute tosser. And generally people who drive those cars are. Think back to every couple you've ever seen in a sports car. Have you ever seen them smiling? No. You'd think a young couple in a sixty-thousand-pound car would be smiling and laughing and full of the joys of a stress-free life. But they always look like they've just had a massive row. As though she's just told him she's pregnant, and he's said, 'Don't worry, I know a great abortionist, I send all my girls to him!' This might be because the immediate instinct of people, when they get in a sports car, is to pose. It's on with the shades, suck in the cheeks, look like you're ready to have sex with someone on the bonnet right now. But too much of that and you look like a poser. Basically, these are the main types of people who drive expensive cars:

- People with too much money, like footballers, city workers and people with inherited wealth. They're revolting because they don't have any sense of proportion or value when it comes to money. Definitely uncool.
- People who have recently come into a little bit of money and want to give the impression they're like people in the

125

above category. I'm talking soap stars and members of boy bands. They're uncool because they're talentless, grasping morons.

- People who have gone bankrupt or got divorced and are living in them so as not to give them up. Very, very uncool.

So go for something anonymous but stylish. Remember, it's more how you behave in car rather than what it is that will determine your cool status. Just pay attention to the following:

- Don't tap the roof in time to music. It's the driving equivalent of air guitaring with a tennis racket in plain view.
- Don't play any of the following on the stereo: Chris de Burgh, the theme from *Miami Vice*, Gary Glitter, Europe, soundtrack to the films *Top Gun*, *Cocktail*, *Pretty Woman* and *Doom*, or compilation albums with titles like *Driving Rock*, *Soft Metal Classics* and *Highway Hits and Motorway Moods*.
- Don't wear gloves or a hat while driving. Unless you're Inspector Frost.

How to be Cool When You're the Driver and Everyone Around You is Drunk

Well, the passengers are probably not going to remember how you behave, so it doesn't matter too much what you do. It's more about how to retain the feeling of cool within yourself. It's difficult when you're surrounded by people breaking wind, opening the window to be sick or begging you to stop so they can go to the toilet. Drunk people can be incredibly annoying – they're loud, obnoxious and talk way to close to you face. Keep your inner cool by allowing your imagination a free rein. You could try playing one of the following scenarios in your head:

- You're flying the last chopper out of 'Nam. These people are sick and wounded, you need to focus on getting them the proper medical attention (toast at home).
- You're behind the Iron Curtain and have spent the night pretending to get drunk with a prominent member of the KGB and his entourage, who you will now start pumping for information.
- You are a Roman centurion and have let your troops cut loose after the final victory of a campaign against the Goth tribes of Germania. You are now charioting them back to camp, ready to sober up in preparation for the long march back to Rome.

- You're the song-writing genius behind a hot new band whose love of rock'n'roll excess will see them implode under a welter of alcoholism and drug addiction which simultaneously sets you free for the mammoth solo career those around have predicted since day one. Of course you'll care for your former bandmates, in the form of clinic fees and mortgage deposits, and in the case of the guitarist, whose pride forces him to refuse handouts, an overly-generous co-writing credit for a song idea he started which you turned into gold and which will act as his pension in the lean years ahead.

- You're the beloved naval captain of a frigate during the Napoleonic Wars and are rowing a band of hand-picked crewman back to your ship after an undercover rum session at a Jamaican port where you picked up vital information about a band of French privateers who have been troubling the fleet.

How to be Cool at a Service Station

Let's be clear, there is nothing cool about service stations. Not the locations, the food, the items on sale, the arcade games, the staff, the décor, the toilets. Zero. No one wants to be there. From the man clearing up the piss stains on the floor to the mother of two working behind the counter on a

Sunday night, to you the motorist, who just wants to be home like everyone else, not eating crap and listening to the inane witterings of regional DJs. So show some love! Talk to the man cleaning the toilets. Not in such a way that he feels compelled to call the police and accuse you of soliciting. But in a way that means he has some real human contact that day. Chat to the woman on the till, express regret that she has to work late on a weekend. Maybe let them keep the change? What you most want to leave is the image of someone who is cool in the sense that they are unaffected. There's nothing cool about looking down on people, nothing cool about aloofness. People mistake that for cool, but it isn't. There's no point in going 'Four pounds for a sandwich?! You people make me sick!' They don't make the prices and they hear that every day. So surprise them.

If that isn't enough to make you feel cool, let your imagination top up your cool tanks. Pretend you're a cop who's driven miles out of his way to meet an informant away from prying eyes. Or a prince in disguise who wants to see how his subjects really live, without the biased filter of his courtiers. Or a writer researching a book or film set amongst low-paid late-night workers.

How to be Cool when Kids are Throwing Sweets at Your Head in the Cinema

Today's kids are very similar to urban foxes – increasingly bold and I'd like to see them chased by dogs. It's a reasonable assumption that, if you go to a weekend or holiday showing of a film, there will be kids talking on their phones, shouting at each other, running up and down, and if you're sitting in front of them, quite possibly chucking various forms of confectionery at your head. The cool thing to do is to tell them in no uncertain terms to stop. But it's only cool if they comply out of a mixture of fear and respect. It's not cool if, as is likely, they intensify their attack on you, mixing the hail of confectionery with insults and even physical blows. No matter how tempting it is, it is even less cool if you start trying to beat the shit out of a group of kids, especially if you come off worse. Other uncool responses to be avoided include:

- Calling the manager. This looks uncool because you're asking for help, plus it will only make it worse. Either they tell off the kids and you get two minutes respite before they renew their attacks, or they throw the kids out and they either wait for you and attack you in the car park or they lodge a fake claim of sexual assault and ruin your career and social life.
- Throwing sweets back at them.

Since the only cool response involves the frankly dream scenario of kids behaving at the request of a stranger, it's best to avoid seeing the kind of films where this sort of behaviour is likely to flourish. Such as

- Teen 'comedies' about intercourse or defecation
- Sequels to films you've never heard of
- Anything starring a former kickboxing champion
- Anything featuring actors playing multiple roles involving fat suits, e.g. *The Nutty Professor, The Nutty Professor 2: The Klumps, Big Momma's House, Big Momma's House 2, Norbit*

This will also help with your cool quotient, as most of these films are frankly dreadful.

How to be Cool When Complaining about Customer Service

This is nigh on impossible given the gibbons that seem to man the phones and desks of most high-street businesses. The thing is, it's not cool to blame the people on the front desk. No one wants to be a Currys Customer Services Agent. Where's the romance in that? It's much cooler, not to say fairer, to keep it as pleasant and as charming as possible. You're not having a go at them, you know they don't make the rules, etc. Here's a quick guide –

'Hello. I'm ringing because the [toaster/computer/car] you sold me is broken.'

Here are their possible responses:

1 They take your name and details
2 They ask you to repeat what you said and still can't quite grasp what you're on about
3 They put you on hold

If you get response 1, proceed to the next stage. If you get 2 or 3, persevere until you get response 1. To keep cool and not turn into a venomous spluttering maniac is quite a challenge, but can be done if you imagine yourself as Harrison Ford in one of the Jack Ryan films of the mid to late 90s. You're a special agent hanging on the phone for a lead that will help track a rogue agent attempting to smuggle fissile material into the United States. To lose your temper will blow your cover and scare off your contact. It helps make it bearable.

Once you've got response 1 and they've taken your details, one of three things will happen:

1 They will deal with your complaint free of
  charge
2 They will deal with your complaint and charge
  you a seemingly unjustifiable and random fee
3 Nothing

Again, you need to get response 1. If you get 2 or 3, keep
it polite and keep on their level, i.e. 'it's not you it's the
system'. Then ask for their name and explain you're doing
a check on customer service standards for a prime-time
BBC show. That should get things moving. Again, while
you're waiting for the gears to grind on, keep yourself
feeling loose and cool by imagining that instead of trying
to get a refund on a kettle, you're dealing with an
incompetent government agency who are trying to cover
up the Prime Minister's son's killing of a homeless man in
a drink drive incident. You're a rugged journalist, think
Gabriel Byrne in *Defence Of The Realm*. Other cool perso-
nas to adopt to take it away from the reality of consumer
angst include:

- Secret agent listening in on coded exchange
- Rock star tracking down old song-writing partner who
  now works in sales
- Exiled king trying to get in touch with loyal aide-de-
  camp to stage restorative coup

Losing your temper is only cool when it's justified, or when you have an audience. Screaming down a phone never feels cool, especially not when you're complaining on the phone to someone who can't or won't do anything about it, because you never get any closure. All you get is a little star next to your name and a starring role in a staff-training module on 'How To Deal With An Aggressive And Unreasonable Customer'.

THE UNCOOLEST ALBUM IN THE WORLD

Songs From The Crystal Cave by Steven Seagal

How to be Cool Getting Out of a Fight

Men are supposed to able to fight, to run away is a dent in anyone's masculinity. It might not be the cool option, but it is the sensible one: who wants to risk getting punched in the face? To get out of it and retain your coolness, you have to give the impression you're tougher than the other guy[s], and that, by trying to call it off, you're saving them a humiliating beating. You could do this by saying the following:

- 'Let's even it up, you can use whatever weapons you like.'
- 'We're agreed, though, the police never get to hear about what I'm about to do to you?'
- 'This is going to last one minute and ten seconds. Because I'm going to give you a minute's worth of free punches.'
- 'Someone film this on their phone. I want this on YouTube under the banner "Me giving an awesome arse-kicking"!'
- 'You really think it's fair to make your mother come down to the morgue?'
- 'Let's do this, I'm looking for a reason to get bounced back to the joint!'

Of course, if you're dealing with someone genuinely hard, these will backfire. In which case, run, throwing money over your shoulder as you go.

How to be Cool When Waiting for a Bus

There are two ways to go on this. You can look calm and collected, yet absorbed. You do this by reading a book. But not any old crap. No titles like *Devil's Conundrum*, *Nexus Berlin*, *Sally's Wedding* or *Rommel's Dogs*. Something cool

- Penguin classics, anything French, something on the Booker shortlist. The other option is to look alert, like you need to be somewhere. You're important! Where is this bus, goddamn it! That way people around you might think you're a big-time lawyer or film director, or the behind-the-scenes person at an international rescue organisation. Or there's the middle ground of the iPod. If you're listening to something uncool, don't worry, they probably can't hear it over the street hubbub. But remember not to sing along. Nothing will puncture your cool like people turning round to stare at you singing 'Boys, boys, boys! I'm looking for a good time!' far louder than you'd imagined. And one final point – don't start a conversation with someone standing next to you, that's just weird.

How to be Cool When on your Phone on a Crowded Bus or Train

When mobile phones first emerged in the 80s, the people who owned and used them were characterised as braying yuppies desperate to stamp their importance on any social situation by yelling into a plastic house-brick. Now that everyone has one, that stigma has gone, but there is still an etiquette to their use and a coolness to be gained or lost.

People react in one of three ways when their phone goes off on public transport. They either:

- Drop the call. This is a 'neutral cool' course of action. It could be cool in that it shows you're too busy lost in your own thoughts to communicate with another being. Or perhaps you're in conversation with someone and don't want to lose the thread. It would be kind of uncool, although understandable, if you dropped the call because you were worried that the kids behind you might start mimicking your speech. Or that you were convinced you were on a bus full of thieves who would then relieve you of your phone, possibly your wallet, and definitely your dignity.
- Take the call in a hushed tone. It's pretty uncool, because you're showing a fear of your environment and that you're cowed. But it's cooler than the third and final reaction.
- Take the call at the top of your voice. Uncool. Cool is about elegance, reserve, respect. Not behaving with the same level of disregard for those around you as a London punk in an 80s Disney film.

So, basically, there's no hard and fast rule here. It depends on the nature of the call and the social make-up of the people around you. And the avoidance of the following phrases, even in jest:

- 'You're through to Mission Control'
- 'If you ever want to see your family again, do exactly as I say'
- 'The hit is on'
- 'You sold me queer giraffes'

How to Have a Cool Ringtone

If you want a cool ringtone, choose the sound of a phone ringing. It's not particularly cool, but it's nowhere near as uncool as all the theme tunes, sound effects and chart hits that fill the air of the modern urban environment like the last demented whimpers of a mad, dying king, sick with fever, rotten with venereal diseases, beloved by no one, whose long-awaited death will set his long-suffering subjects free from the yoke of his idiotic tyranny. You think I'm overreacting? You sit on a bus three times a day in London and see if you don't think we're about to implode. Why would someone think it's OK to play music out of their phone speakers in public? How would they like it if the person next to them started reading their book aloud? I'm sure they'd love to hear about the Persian Wars of the fifth century BC about as much as everyone else wants to hear the snarlings of some over-hyped gun-toting sex-obsessed no-dick, i.e. not at all.

How to Be Cool When Standing Under a Streetlight

This all depends on why you're standing under a streetlight. Here are some cool reasons:

- You're a private eye shadowing a millionaire's wife he thinks is having an affair. And now you've gone and fallen in love with her.
- You're being painted for your album cover.
- You're being photographed for the front of *Vogue*, to go with the caption 'The Hottest Star In Britain'.
- You're looking in on your kids getting ready for bed. You don't want to trouble your ex-wife, you just want to know they're OK and let them know that daddy's going off on one last mission from which he may not return.
- You're a spy. But one of those nice honourable ones from a John Le Carré novel. Not one of those poisoning Russian bastards.

And here are some not so cool reasons to be standing under a streetlight:

- You're stalking someone

- You're scared of the dark and so are waiting in the light till someone rescues you
- You're relieving yourself against the streetlight
- You fix streetlights

How to Be Cool When You've Been Arrested

Of course in films this is very cool indeed. And in real life it can be an aid to coolness, certainly it never harmed Paul McCartney or Pete Doherty: it helps with the bad boy image. Ultimately, it depends on the crime you're accused of. Cool ones are:

- Some kind of disturbance. Nothing actually violent, maybe a fracas at a nightspot
- Embezzlement from a large firm for purposes of redistribution to the poor
- Cat burglary

It should be pointed out that the coolness gained by you committing the first two are largely dependent on you being famous in the first place. And any other crimes are deeply uncool. But if you're in the cells for the above and you feel your cool enhanced, just make sure you don't start blubbing about your innocence or fall to your knees begging forgiveness from whatever deity you can remember. Give it the strong, silent, no big deal reaction.

How to Be Cool in Prison

Well, this depends on the crime, but let's presume you're either in for a crime you didn't commit, or for something white collar. Now, in popular culture, the cool things to do in prison include:

- Press-ups
- A levels
- Arts and crafts
- Learning new languages
- Teaching other inmates to read
- Putting on plays
- Befriending the guards
- Proving your innocence

In reality, I think we all know that you're looking at a regime of beatings, regular privations and occasional sodomy. The way to be cool amidst such a nightmare scenario is to hide in your cell and keep your head down. And remember, any sign of weakness will be exploited. So

How to be Cool . . .

DO – Treat those around you with respect

and

DON'T – Offer them a leading role in the Christmas panto in return for protection

URBAN ENVIRONMENT COOLOMETER TEST

1 **You take a swig from a beer bottle and spill some down your front. Do you**

a) Start screaming 'Mother was right! I'm such a fucking loser! I'm such a fucking loser!' as you smash yourself round the head with the bottle

b) Rip off your top saying 'Damn thing needed a wash anyway, now who wants to suck on my titties?'

c) Dab it off with a napkin or tissue

d) Pour the rest of the contents over your head saying 'Y'all so square in here! Where's the motherfuckin' atmosphere, you chicken shit pumpernickels?'

2 **You are in a bar when someone selects 'Walk This Way' by Aerosmith and Run DMC on the jukebox. Do you**

a) Lick the contents of an ashtray in time to the music

b) Start complaining loudly that all banks are run by Jews

c) Hail it as a great rock/rap crossover

d) Jump up on the bar and walk along it like Genesis in the 'We Can't Dance' video, encouraging others to do the same

3 You chance upon George Clooney coming out of a club in London's West End. Do you

a) Swoon in his arms saying 'Ooh, Doctor Ross, can you check my poopy pants?'

b) Say 'Your looks and charm will fade like a badger's scent from a gassed set'

c) Smile politely and continue on your way

d) Slow clap and declaim loudly 'Big fuckin' thrills! It's George fuckin' Clooney! Whoopie fuckin' doo!'

4 A group of women on a hen night scream at you from the confines of a white limo. Do you

a) Climb on top of the car and piss on them through the sunroof

b) Wipe your arse on all the notes in your wallet and throw them at them shouting 'You are filth!'

c) Ignore them whilst pretending to read a text on your phone

d) Walk up to them singing 'You've Lost That Loving Feeling' and removing items of clothing as you go

5 You pass a building site as some builders whistle at an attractive girl. Do you

a) Drop to all fours and say 'Ride me like a dirty pony!'

b) Start climbing the scaffolding while saying 'I'm climbing skyward to the hot boy party'

c) Ignore them

d) Start knocking the base of the scaffolding and yelling 'Come and do that to her face, you pussies!'

If you answered mainly 'a', you have all the cool and charm of a fight in a chip-shop queue over whose turn it is to use the ketchup.

If you answered mainly 'b', bad news. You know when people talk about scum that shit and shag in doorways? That's you.

If you answered mainly 'c', you can look cool in a city. As long as it's not Leicester. Don't go back there!

If you answered mainly 'd', I'd move to a farm. Not to grow organic veg, but so that the animals get to feel superior.

Chapter 7
HOW TO BE COOL . . .
ON HOLIDAY

It's tempting, when you're away from work, to let everything go, but your coolness must be retained. Even though you'll never see a lot of the people you meet again, they're still an audience worth playing to. Unless you're going on a Club 18–30 holiday, in which case you deserve everything you get. Including syphilis and the loss of your wallet.

How to Be Cool When Having Your Hand Baggage Searched

It's never that cool having your hand baggage searched. For a start, you tend to look at the people doing it and think 'This is the front line against terrorism? This is the best we can do? These overweight fifty-somethings who are too good for shelf-stacking, but not good enough to be running a Little Chef?' It's cool to be polite to them and act like you're a well-seasoned traveller who's used to these procedures. But for a real cool glow, you need to use your imagination. Pretend you're one of the following:

- A spy who's returning with valuable information concealed on a microfilm hidden in your toothpaste

- An agent hired to test airport security, and you're privately unhappy that they haven't spotted that your iPod is full of fake semtex
- An undercover officer travelling incognito in order to identify and disarm potential hijackers

How to Be Cool When Your Flight is Delayed

This is such dead time, there's very little in the way of cool activities to undertake. You can waste ten pounds on a raffle to win a car that never seems to get won. You can eat a sandwich from any number of high-street outlets. You can spend fifteen pounds on a discus-like pizza in a fake and pointless 'authentic' bar. You could even dine at one of the wildly inappropriate seafood bars that seem to have sprung up in all the major British airports. On the surface, these are actually quite cool. They're very sleek, you can order wine or champagne, you can pretend you in a Mediterranean bar. But they are inappropriate because they're in an airport miles from the sea. It's never quite going to have that 'Catch of the Day' freshness. So why take the risk of spending the flight and the first few days of the holidays going off at both ends like a fire hydrant when there are other less obvious ways of feeling cool.

- Get someone to teach you the rudiments of their language
- Organise a discussion forum for people from opposing religious groups
- Get people's numbers after telling them you're a modelling agent and you think they have a great look

How to Be Cool on a Long-Haul Flight

Well, the way to be really cool on a long-haul flight is to travel business class. But who can afford that on a regular basis? The kind of money those seats cost, and the actual value they represent, make you want to pay with a briefcase stuffed full of cash exchanged in a car park. The thing about travelling business class is that you have to make it look like you do it all the time. Don't let slip that it's a real treat, people will think you're mad spending money on a nine-hour flight that could give you a new bathroom or pay for a hit on a minor member of the cabinet.

Most of us are stuck in economy, with no legroom and crappy food making it hard to feel like a film or rock star. It's definitely not cool to:

- Emit noxious body odours
- Bore the person next to you with unasked for anecdotes about your family and friends

- Give your own director's commentary on whatever film you're watching
- Say to everyone who passes 'Do you want to join the Mile High Club?'

In truth, like a wedding of a friend of your partner's you don't really know, it's there to be sat out.

How to Be Cool at Baggage Reclaim

Here you have to strike a balance between looking like you have places to go and not looking desperate. So don't stand peering down the flap where the bags come through. Be in the area, and then go in for your bag when you see it. It also looks cool if you help the elderly with their bags if they look too heavy. And it's important not to:

- Knock people over as you lunge in a panic for your bag and drag it back to your trolley
- Get into a fight over ownership of similar-looking bags
- Joke with people of Middle Eastern appearance that they must have 'called off the operation!'

How to Be Cool When Walking Out of the Arrivals Hall

The only way to look really cool is to walk straight up to the flashest looking person with a sign, i.e. not a minicab driver with a hastily scrawled felt-tip name on the back of an envelope he found on the floor. I mean a suited-and-booted-looking chauffeur. Walk up to them in full view of everyone, shake hands with them so everyone thinks they're there to pick you up, and keep talking to them till everyone on your flight has passed you, then just ask the chauffeur directions to the toilet and continue on your way.

COOL HIDDEN TALENTS
Musician, painter, pilot, astronaut
UNCOOL HIDDEN TALENTS
Maggot farmer, pornographer, torturer, Scientologist

How to Be Cool on a Beach

It's a lot of pressure on the beach. It's the most naked most of us ever get in public. A couple of things are obvious to avoid if coolness is to be maintained:

- Pointing at other people's bodies in a positive or negative manner
- Going to the toilet, even if you bury it
- The pulling down of other people's costumes
- The chat-up line 'Didn't I see you on *Baywatch*?'
- Getting changed under a homemade neck to ankle towel tepee

The cool rules are:

- Sunglasses at all times, except in the sea
- Cool towels, i.e. nothing with a silhouette of a busty girl in front of a flaming sun and the logo 'Florida 100% hot'
- Cool trunks. That means anything except speedos and pouches
- Use suntan lotion. Sunburn says 'beach amateur' in the same way that driving gloves say 'retired Nazi'

How to Be Cool in an Art Gallery

Visiting an art gallery always seems like such a good idea. And it is, they generally look like a really cool places to go. But forty minutes in and you start to think 'There are a lot of paintings here, my brain has turned to mush.' Keep going, just stick to these viewing methods and everyone around will think you know what you're looking at:

- Intent stare married with slow stroke of the chin with your hand
- Intrigued tilt of the head to show really serious contemplation
- Stepping back and forth to view the painting from several distances
- A crouch. This is optional, but shows deep thought and reverence for the work in question

On no account ask anyone else a question! Look like you know it all. For extra cool, you could carry round a notebook and intermittently scribble in it. It doesn't matter if it's rubbish, you could be writing 'He's got a great arse!' or the lyrics to 'Let's Get Ready To Rumble', no one's ever going to read it, but to the casual observer you'll look like a deep and committed fan of the arts.

How to Be Cool as a Brit Abroad on Holiday

Now here's a challenge. There are a number of countries where we, and by 'we' I mean 'Britons', left a bit of a mess. The dinner party equivalent of nicking some CDs and copping a feel of the host's wife. Sometimes this behaviour was centuries ago, i.e. the Empire, sometimes it's more recent, i.e. scummy British tourists in Spain, Greece, etc. The best way to be cool in these situations is, for a start, to play it down. So no

- Union Jack shorts
- Singing in fountains
- Baring of the buttocks at local womenfolk or members of the constabulary
- Vomiting/urinating in streets/hotel foyers/shops
- Intimations as to the true sexuality of local males

All of this is not only deeply uncool behaviour, it also says 'Hello, I'm from the British Isles.' It's exactly the sort of thing that has made us so unpopular in vast swathes of Europe. And is curious, given our clearly undeserved reputation for politeness. Now, generally speaking, if you keep your head down and don't draw attention to yourself, that's the uncool bomb diffused.

There's also the good news that, in some parts of the world, they love the British! I'm talking mainly about America. You might not believe this, but we're already cool over there, before we've even done anything! You know how most Americans seem infused with cool to us? OK, when I say 'most', I'm excluding the following:

- Fat ones
- Ones in denim shirts, chinos, naval baseball caps and aviation shades
- Ones wearing their just-researched tartan
- Ones who are either members or fans of goth metal bands that make videos where CGI beetles crawl under people's skin and turn their eyes black
- Ones who are in bands when they're in their thirties, but dress like they're in their twenties, and make music for teenagers which involves pogoing in outsize shorts to songs about how they want to bone their best friend's mom
- Ones who dispute evolution and belong to some sort of Christian Right militia
- Ones who talk about countries like Arabland and Pakistania
- Ones who start unfounded pre-emptive wars

But it's a big place, so there's a whole load of people left who don't fit on that list. Americans are still cool. Most cool icons are American. It has the romance of the Wild West, jazz, blues, rock'n'roll and Hollywood. OK, so that exchange student you met has nothing in any real sense to do with that. He just has long hair and a sexy drawl. But most of us don't know the Queen or drink tea every day at four on the dot, but Americans certainly think we do. So why not fulfil their stereotyped image of you! Here are some ways you, as a Brit, can appear even cooler when in America:

- Simply use your voice. They love it! Even an accent considered uncool in your own country, such as Home Counties or Chelsea, sounds super-sexy-cool to them. They'll think you're a cross between Hugh Grant and James Bond. And if you have a regional accent, that's a bonus too: they'll think you sound like The Beatles!
- Allude to being distantly related to royalty
- Take a picture of a National Trust thatched cottage and pretend it's your house
- Use words like 'ghastly', 'super', 'blimey' and 'tickety-boo'

So that's it – pipe down on the European seaboard, play it normal everywhere else, and pipe up in America.

How to Be Cool When Presented with a Local Delicacy that Turns Your Stomach

Snails, snake, bits of frog, brains. If you're on holiday and you're not familiar with the language the menu is written in, you could very easily end up with one of these objects on your plate. But by then it's too late. The cool traveller is open to new experiences. You can't fling it back at them screaming 'Jesus Christ, you people are fucking savages!' So tuck in. Best-case scenario: it's surprisingly pleasant and you can launch a new career as an exotic food importer. Worst-case scenario: you've got a great cool anecdote. Actually, another worse-case scenario is that you get horrendous food poisoning, or contract some rare disease that baffles the doctors when you get home. So, fingers crossed.

How to Be Cool When Going Round a National Trust Property

It's a bank holiday, you're at your parents, or your partner's parents. If you're middle class, you go round a National Trust property. It's cool to

- Show a wide-ranging knowledge of history
- Smile and be considerate towards old people
- Remark upon the beautiful gardens

It's not so cool to

- Try to hide in a suit of armour
- Roll your eyes and talk about how much the country's changed every time you see someone from a lower class or different ethnic background
- Steal a pile of tea towels

How to Be Cool at a Music Festival

Another bank holiday activity is the music festival. Music festivals have changed in recent years. Originally the preserve of students and 'travelling folk', by which I mean fans of The Levellers as opposed to Romanies, they are now a rite of passage for every middle-class professional couple. Now you may find it a fearfully intimidating prospect, but just relax and embrace the event and you'll have a great time, plus you get loads of cool points for having attended. As long as you don't:

- Say 'Mmm, I love the smell of chemical toilets!'
- Walk round with a compass and a map of the grounds hanging round your neck in a plastic folder
- Wake up on the first day, say 'Fuck this!', and check into the nearest hotel
- Go on and on about how rubbish the bill is, adding 'Best band I've ever seen live? Huey Lewis and the News'

UNCOOL LOOK
Suit on a beach, dungarees at a ball, shorts at a funeral

If you're a bit younger and single, then the way to have a really cool festival is to abandon all social norms. You can

- Drink at breakfast
- Wrestle nude in the mud with a stranger
- Go and see a World Music act and feel really 'authentic'
- Take a photo of someone on your phone who you think once presented something on T4

HOLIDAY COOLOMETER TEST

1 You're on holiday when someone local asks you where you're from. Do you

a) Say 'My papers are in order' and run away zig-zagging like you're trying to avoid sniper fire

b) Say 'I'll tell you were I'm from, pal. A place that taught your lot to use a knife and fork'

c) Tell them the truth

d) Say 'A little bit of Narnia, a little bit of the Shire, and a whole lotta love!'

2 You're lying on a beach when a kid frantically digging a hole accidentally showers you in sand. Do you

a) Bury the kid up to their neck in sand and leave after having put a bucket over their head

b) Call the local directory service and demand the number for a 'child catcher'

c) Ask them to stop chucking sand at you and then build them an amazing sandcastle

d) Start dancing down the beach singing Bob Marley's 'Three Little Birds'

3 Your flight is delayed indefinitely. Do you

a) Claim you need to get to your destination immediately so as to obtain the antidote to the slow-acting poison administered to you by enemies of the realm

b) Try and sneak on another flight disguised as a baggage handler

c) Spend the time reading a book

d) Only communicate using lines from *Top Gun*

4 You find yourself at the same hotel as someone you slightly know and barely like. Do you

a) Hire some local toughs to warn them to stay away from you

b) Tell the hotel staff you've seen them taking a recording device into the toilets

c) Be polite and friendly, but maintain a distance

d) Say 'Let's cut the crap. You don't like me, I don't give a shit about you. Doesn't mean we can't have a drink. Although I am busy from now till my death'

**5 You're in the queue for the toilets at a music festival.
Do you**

a) Take a survey of what bodily functions people intend to
partake of in the cubicles but shout 'Wrong!' whatever
they answer

b) Keep asking 'Are these good ones? Are they worth
queuing for? Should I have brought my camera?'

c) Strike up a conversation about which bands people have
seen so far

d) Try to break the record for the most number of people
crammed in a toilet, which predictably results in a literal
shower of shit

If you answered mainly 'a', the locals would rather
welcome the entire Russian army to their country than
you and your family.

If you answered mainly 'b', the only good thing about you
going on holiday is that it gives your colleagues and
neighbours a rest.

If you answered mainly 'c', you are a fine ambassador for cool
and the country. Until they find that box under your bed!

If you answered mainly 'd', unless you see foreign prisons
and the bribing of local policemen primarily as a good
source of anecdotes, I'd stay at home.

Chapter 8
HOW TO BE COOL . . .
IN RELATIONSHIPS

This is why we do it. Cool is about projecting sex in order to get it. Not literally, don't make a sign with what you're prepared to do and for how much. A lot of it is unsaid.

How to Be Cool When There's Immediate Attraction on the First Meeting

The rule for both sexes seems to be – be attentive but act like you don't care at the same time. So for women the message would be something like 'I-find-you-fascinating-and-sexual-but-I've-got-plenty-lined-up-so-make-up-your-mind-quick-slow-down-stranger-I-hardly-know-you-give-me-some-commitment-stop-it's-moving-too-fast'. For men it's more complex. If she's looking for bad boy danger, imply you are highly sexed and that women find you untameable, but don't go as far as 'I'm thinking of getting an Aids test.' If she's looking for a husband, just roll out the usual nonsense like 'For me, commitment is the greatest aphrodisiac.' In fact, if you combine the two approaches, you are ultra-cool – 'If I wanted a quick fuck, I could get that walking into any bar in town. But you, you're different. I would never get bored with making love to you.'

How to Be Cool When Chatting Up a Woman

This is what cool is all about – sexual allure and potency. You've got to look like it's no big deal. Even if she won't give you her number, you've still enjoyed talking to her, there's no agenda here, you're just enjoying the company of a beautiful intelligent woman. Make sure you are, by the way. Avoid high-maintenance mentalists by spotting these signs:

- Long-term single in their late thirties. Their friends will say 'I can't understand it! She's so great, there just aren't any men good enough for her out there!' But come on, really, there must be *something* wrong with her.
- If they make it difficult for you to approach them through excessive scorn and sarcasm. Now you may be making a fool of yourself by drunkenly dribbling about how they're like Fearne Cotton, but not as hot, in which case you deserve everything you get. But if you're being polite and attentive and they're treating you like a morris dancer at a biker's convention, then don't see it as a challenge, cut your losses and leave them to their lonely bitter selves.
- Desperate, i.e. asks for details of your financial status and sperm count.

If you think the ground is clear of those nightmares, proceed. Now I'm not talking about chatting up a woman for a one-night stand, that's a whole other set of issues and it doesn't normally concern cool as much as opportunity. Most men would fuck a stray dog if they could get it to keep still. If that is what you want, then skip to the 'One Stop Cool Shop' at the end of this book. But here I'm talking about chatting up a woman you really want to have a relationship with. The kind of drunken tart who'll bang a stranger on a bin isn't going to be impressed by your knowledge of nineteenth-century German literature or the fact you can name her perfume. This is a different kind of woman – classy, bright, worth fighting for. She can spot cheap shots, so you've got to be extra-schooled in cool.

First off, play the urbane man about town. Get yourself a well-cut suit. Not something two sizes too big from Oxfam, and 3-for-the-price-of-2 ties from an outlet in a train-station. Splash out on a classic suit, you won't regret it. Now that you look the part, you have to sound the part. No swearing. Why would you need to swear in front of a woman like that? 'You're single? You're shitting me!' 'Fuck me, you're hot!' No. Sophistication is cool, crudity isn't. Then you have to talk up what you do. Supposing you work in retail, or a nondescript office job, no matter. You want a straight nine-to-five so that you can have enough time to finish your play, or your book, or to develop your photos. If you don't have anything in your life like this, get something.

You must have an interest! Pursue it to an esoteric degree. Whatever you do, don't make something up you have no interest in or knowledge of, you will get found out. Build on something you know about. But don't lay it out too blatantly. Don't begin with 'I'm Dave, I work in Topshop but I write plays. I'm really sensitive, see!' It's much cooler that they draw it out of you, or it looks like you let it slip. They mustn't feel like you're playing them. And you're not, that's really uncool. I'm not giving you one of those dodgy dating guides where you lie and connive your way into bed. Women don't find that cool, and other men will hate you because they don't have the balls to do it. Cool must be played straight. If it doesn't come easy, grow into it so it feels like a part of you. Here are some cool attributes:

- Doting on nephews, nieces and godchildren is cool. It shows you're not afraid to have kids
- Learn to cook
- Play an instrument
- Be up to date with current affairs

How to Be Cool When Chatting Up a Man

This is pretty damn easy – make it clear you want to sleep with him. Cool!

How to Be Cool on a First Date

First impressions count for so much, so take it easy. As a man, it's important to impress upon her that you're someone of sophistication and means. So take her to a classy restaurant, but be aware that, if it develops into a relationship, you might be setting the bar too high. It can be cool to play it casual, to put her at her ease. A top restaurant might make her nervous, put her under pressure. Don't go too far the other way, though. Champagne and chips works great in an advert, but in reality most people's reactions would be 'You've got to be fucking joking!' Putting them under pressure to sleep with you is definitely the uncoolest thing you can do. In spite of that, most men seem to think there's a sliding scale of sexual favours they can expect in return for what they lay on on the first date, i.e.

- Drinks: kissing
- Dinner at medium restaurant: groping
- Dinner at fashionable nightspot: the works

It's much cooler just to enjoy the night and make it clear you don't expect anything in return, but you're happy if it's there.

Now for the ladies. It's imperative that you don't do any of the following on a first date if you wish to come across as cool:

- Talk about your ex-boyfriends
- Start crying about how you're never going to get married
- Ask how many children he'd ideally like
- Demand to see his diary for the next month
- Bring up whose parents you should spend Christmas with

Neediness is not cool. If he's there, he likes you. You are in control.

How to Be Cool on a Date in a Restaurant

Ordering in the language of the cuisine is always impressive. As is being adventurous with your menu choices. And sound like you know about wine, quite an easy one to bluff – just throw in words like 'bouquet' and 'tannins' then go for the third cheapest. It's sometimes cool to ask the advice of the waiter, although not 'How's the body language – should I suggest coffee at mine?'

If you're on a date, make it sound like you go to a lot of restaurants, but that you don't throw the same moves on every date. Take the lead from your date. If they fancy a starter or pudding but you don't, say 'Go ahead, I don't mind!' You do mind, obviously, who wants to watch someone else eat? But you can't say 'Hold off, fatty, how about we don't eat everything in the kitchen!'

Here are some other things it is not cool to do in a restaurant:

- Order a second pudding
- Send food back more than once. I don't care if they bring you a cowpat, you eat it
- Split the bill exactly according to who ate and drank what, down to who had more glasses of wine from each bottle
- Play on your portable PlayStation
- Steal cutlery
- Do a runner

How to Be Cool When You Find Yourself in a Restaurant Way Out of Your Price Range

First up, a definite no – don't go to the toilet and try to crawl out of the window. You have to suck it up and pay. In fact, more than that, you have to pay as though you're used to spending that kind of money. So no rolling of eyes or mouthing of 'Jesus Christ!' as you look at the menu. No 'I better go and check my balance' or 'Do you mind if we go halves tonight, it's just, what with the rent and the gas bill, I'm a little tight right now.' No 'Ooh, I'm not that hungry, how about we just share a starter and have some tap water?' No 'You better put out after this!' And definitely no 'These c**ts are seriously mistaken if they think they're getting a tip at these fucking prices!' No, the cool man or woman about town doesn't bat an eyelid, reaches for their credit card, utters a silent prayer that it goes through, then sobs themselves to sleep at the thought that they'll have to sell a kidney to pay off the debt.

How to Be Cool When Receiving an Unwanted Serenade in a Restaurant

Picture the scene – you're in a restaurant, enjoying a romantic evening with the love of your life. At no point are either of you thinking 'What I'd really like now is for a stranger to come and sing at me.' So why the hell do restaurant managers book these acts? It's agony, everyone in the room looks at you, and you don't know what to do. Are you supposed to keep eating and ignore them? Sit and watch them, letting your food go cold? Clap along? Dance? Sing back at them? What are the rules? Specifically, what are the cool rules? Well, in a cool world, you'd pull out an instrument and join in, to the delight of the rest of the restaurant, who'd be on their feet in no time, cheering you on in your virtuoso display while your date looked on glowing with pride and desire. But that's about as likely as a 'sorry' from George Bush. The achievably cool way to do deal with it is to sit and smile through it, then, when your date looks away, slip the musician twenty pounds and tell them to piss off.

Never, ever do a moonwalk

How to Be Cool When a Waiter or Waitress Accidentally Spills Something On You

First off, you need to be sure it was an accident. There's an easy way to tell. Are you, or have you been behaving like, an arsehole? If the answer's 'no', it was probably a genuine accident. If it's 'yes', they may have done it on purpose, but it'll be hard to prove. It's part of the training of a waiter or waitress to tip wine or gravy down someone who's clearly an insufferable prick and pass it off as an accident. If you deserved it, your course of action should be the same as someone who is blameless. But since you're an arsehole, you'll probably react in one of the following ways:

- Scream at the top of your lungs about how much your shirt/blouse/jacket/skirt cost
- Smash a plate on the floor and demand a written apology
- Smear a similar amount of food or liquid on everyone else's clothes in the restaurant

For the non-arseholes, I recommend one of the following reactions:

- Explain that it's really no bother, you hated that item of clothing anyway, you've been meaning to throw it out, they've done you a favour
- Cheekily use the incident to negotiate a free pudding
- Empathise with them about the hours and stress of their job (NB not to the point where your partner thinks you're hitting on them. But if you're on your own or just with a friend, why not go for it and gently extort a date from them?)

How to Be Cool When Your Partner is Flirting with the Waiter or Waitress

The problem with reacting to your partner flirting with someone else when you don't want them to is that jealousy is a very uncool, unattractive quality. The instinctive reaction is to try to make your partner feel jealous or hurt as well. You can do this in a number of ways. You can

- Make a phone call arranging to have dinner with an ex or with the friend that your partner hates. Trust me, everyone has one of those
- Leave without contributing to the bill
- Attack the waiter/waitress, screaming 'You piece of shit! You're just a fucking waiter!'
- Feign some kind of seizure which allows you to pull the tablecloth off and smash all the plates

But I don't need to tell you that none of this is cool. Now, if the flirting was initiated by your partner, there are obviously some issues in your relationship that need dealing with. They are clearly feeling neglected by you and want your attention. The cool thing to do is to call them on it and apologise if you haven't been there for them recently, you'll make it up to them, etc. Unless they do it all the time, in which case they're mental and you should get rid of them as soon as you can, although be careful, as that might provoke a barrage of abusive texts, emails and generally erratic behaviour.

If the flirting was initiated by the waiter or waitress, and your partner was a polite or unwilling accomplice, it might be tempting to do one of the following:

* Accuse them of cloning your credit card
* When your partner goes to the toilet, put a cigarette butt in their food and summon the manager to complain
* Phone *Crimestoppers* and give a description of them, claiming they're a sex trafficker

But the cool thing is to rise above it. Of course people are going to flirt with your partner, they're really, really hot. It's a compliment!

How to Be Cool in Bed

Being cool in bed is about taking control. Take the lead, give it a sense of urgency and respect. But do not, under any circumstances, adopt the stance or speech patterns of a Nazi tank commander. Trust me. Bad move. It's also not cool to

- Cry
- Laugh
- Point
- Stare

Or to say things like

- 'What do you think you're doing?'
- 'I don't think you're taking this very seriously!'
- 'Make a bloody effort'
- 'You have done this before, right?'
- 'I'd be better off paying for this'
- 'Is that supposed to be turning me on'
- 'Are you trying to break it?'

The key to being cool in bed, as with most things cool, is to take everything in your stride: don't be fazed. That said, there are some positions that it would be uncool to engage in the first time you sleep with someone:

- Them wearing a leash, and you thrashing them with a riding crop
- You tying yourself up then urging them on with cries of 'Treat me like the slut that I am!' or 'I've been such a bad boy. Go on, hurt me, Mummy, I deserve it!'
- In front of a display of pictures of your ex

How to Be Cool When You've Woken Up with Someone You Never Want to See Again

We've all been there, whether it's out of drunken desperation or cold-hearted revenge. But sleeping with someone you either didn't mean to, or don't want to again can be tricky. Especially if you want to look cool. First of all, weigh it up and work out why you don't want to see them again. They could be

- A colleague
- A relative. Not a close one, maybe even only by marriage. But it's one of those 'it's not illegal but it isn't right' scenarios
- Several leagues below you

Now sometimes these things work out of their own accord. But go with your instincts. You'll know whether you want to see them again by your reaction on waking. If you want to throw up or jump out of the window, then I think you know this isn't going to go to a second date. If the thought of your friends finding out makes you want to move abroad, then, again, no point in leaving your number. If they wake and suggest breakfast and you find yourself pretending to take a call informing you of the death of a relative, then who are you kidding? This was a colossal mistake up there with the Poll Tax and *The Avengers* film. You have to get out, and fast! Or do you? What if they're at yours? Either way, you cannot be honest. It might seem quick and easy to say:

- 'I feel disgusted with myself. Goodbye.'
- 'This is just something I've got to learn to live with.'
- 'You tell anyone about this, I swear I will rain down upon you a shit storm the like of which the world has never seen!'
- 'I will pay you anything to deny this ever took place.'

But those are all really uncool reactions. The cool way to play it is 'Hey, that was fun. Must do it again sometime, but I'm kind of busy right now.' They might think you're playing hard to get, but they'll find out you're not just *playing* hard to get, you *are* hard to get. But you can deal with that later. Right now you still have the problem of how to get out of their place, or get them out of yours, with your coolness intact. Now, if it's a workday, that's easy. But if it's a weekend, you're going to need a bit of coaching. Don't use the first thing that comes into your head – doctor's appointment, furniture delivery, catching up on work at home. For one, they might suggest hanging around and helping, or waiting till you're done. Secondly, and more importantly, they're not cool excuses. OK, so you're never going to see this person again. But when they tell their friends about you, you want them to make you sound good. It helps to spread your cool aura. So go with something more like one of these:

- You've got to run twelve miles as part of your training for the marathon
- You're the activities organiser at a local centre for deprived kids
- You're cutting a demo with your band. It's no big deal, just something you do for fun. Your real passion is your writing
- You volunteered to spend the day cleaning up the grounds and gardens of a rough council estate
- It's your shift at The Samaritans

You're home free. Just drop their calls and dodge their date offers. Always with a cool excuse, mind. And if anyone ever asks 'Did you two ever . . . ?' just laugh it off saying 'As if!'

How to Be Cool When Meeting Your Partner's Parents

When a woman meets her boyfriend's parents, she has to convey to the mother that she will look after her little boy, and to the dad that she puts out. When a man meets his girlfriend's parents, he has to convince the mother that he will be faithful and loving to her little girl, and to the dad that he's earning enough to share the cost of a potential wedding. Get that right and they'll welcome you with open arms.

> Bizarrely, Simon Callow is much cooler than Simon Cowell

How to Be Cool With That Friend or Relative of Your Partner's That You Really Don't Like

This is something that happens to us all, and is nothing to feel guilty or ashamed about. Everyone fights it, inside, but we've all encountered some of the following. Men have to put up with:

- Male friend of your girlfriend who's clearly been in love with her for the last ten years and buys her inappropriate gifts, such as perfume and lingerie
- Gay friend of your girlfriend she describes as 'hilarious' and 'so funny', but you find unutterably tiresome and generally unpleasant

- Permanently single friend of your girlfriend who resents you for taking away her best friend

And women have to put up with:

- Laddish best friend of your boyfriend who thinks you've made him 'sell out' because he doesn't want to drink till he pisses blood or throws up in strip club toilets any more
- Possessive ex-girlfriend who demands social priority from your boyfriend. Even though you've been seeing him for two years now, longer than she did. But she'll throw a fit if he spends more on your birthday than hers
- Close male friend of your boyfriend who only talks about football/computer games/films/cars and refuses to include you in any but the most cursory conversations

And both genders may occasionally encounter:

- Mother of partner whose suggestions such as 'Maybe we could see you this weekend' are actually orders that only the foolhardy would disobey
- Single siblings who throw sulks at weddings and christenings, etc. because they're not the centre of attention

Now the majority of evidence, albeit anecdotal, is overwhelmingly in favour of never, ever, *ever* mentioning any of this.

Nothing will be gained from saying 'Maybe the reason your sister is single is because she's overweight and rude?', or 'Does Nick hate me because he's had a massive gay crush on you since school?' Remember that cool is a tolerant state of mind. So put it aside, and face them with a smile.

How to Be Cool When Asking for Someone's Hand in Marriage

This is a tricky one to pull off. Obviously, you have to be sure they'll say yes, which means you're probably in a long term relationship, thus they will be expecting it. But the key to a cool proposal is the element of surprise. Now, you want to wrong foot them and throw them off the scent. Don't do this by letting them find you in bed with someone else, or telling them you need some space while you work out where your life is going. I mean business as usual, then hit them with it sideways. Don't pick an obvious day, like a birthday, Christmas or Valentine's, unless you feel really confident you can pull off a double bluff. This means pretending you've forgotten the day, or haven't planned anything really big. This might, of course, mean you take a shoe to the balls, although that might be a good test of whether you really want to be legally bound to such a violent, needy, egocentric maniac. It's easier to surprise someone when they're not expecting it.

Don't push this too far: they're not going to be expecting it at the graveside of a loved one, or doubled up on a toilet floor after some dodgy tagine at an Egyptian restaurant. So choose a romantic setting like a beach or a riverbank or a classy restaurant. And make the setting seem casual so they don't know what's coming, i.e. don't say 'Let's go for dinner, there's something I need to tell you', they'll think you're leaving them/dying/reconfiguring your sexuality. Elaborate proposals are very romantic, but keep it simple – write it in the sand, for example. Don't try to train a robin to land on her wrist with the ring tied round its neck – worst-case scenario: you're arrested for accidentally strangling a robin. Best-case scenario: she ends up in casualty having a tetanus jab after being bitten trying to get a ring off a robin's neck. And try to limit the number of people involved to just one – you. Getting a friend to light the petrol-written letters 'Will you marry me?' as you walk into a field is hard to time, would need a stepladder to read, and may result in a forest fire that could overshadow your special moment. Likewise, most waiters are out-of-work actors so they might be able to handle instructions, but they're also attention-seekers. The last thing you want is them bumping up their part by reciting a poem or a Shakespeare soliloquy you don't recognise, making your new fiancée realize you're not the sophisticated urban art-lover you've pretended to be. Plus, you can predict the conversation after:

MAN: What a wanker, doing that poem!

WOMAN: I thought it was sweet.

MAN: Well, why don't you marry him then!

WOMAN: Where's this coming from?

MAN: Fuck you, give me the ring back!

So keep it manageable. If you're going for ultra-romance and tradition, you'll want to go down on one knee. Again, this may flag up what you're about to ask her. Now this may be useful as a test, if you're not sure how she feels and her reaction is to say 'For Christ's sake, get up, you're making a fool of yourself!' before you've opened your mouth, then it's back to www.russianbrides.com. But if you're sure it's going to be a yes, i.e. she's dropped hints by bursting into tears every time another of her friends gets engaged and sobbed 'I'm never going to get married, why do you keep me in this purgatory?!', then you don't want her to see it coming. So how do you get down on one knee without her thinking you're about to bankrupt her parents and give her a day so special and exciting it usually leads to a crushing depression that gives every other day the feeling of stultifying predictability? Well there are really only two options:

1 Pretend to tie your shoelace
2 Pretend to tie her shoelace

I cannot stress enough that kneeling down to sniff her shoe because you think she might have trodden in dog shit will mean that a proposal is the last thing she's expecting, and it is not an association that any woman wants with a proposal. And if it was, and she reacted by winking and saying 'Kinky!', then run as fast as you can without looking back until you're across one or more borders.

And please avoid the following uncool ways of proposing:

- Ring hidden in cowpat served as joke on Pancake Day
- With the words 'I don't think I'm going to do any better . . . *(pause for thought)* . . . no, I'm really not. Time for me to cash in my love chips . . .'
- While they're mopping your brow as you heave into a toilet on your return from a friend's stag night
- From the stage of a Meatloaf concert
- To try to calm down an argument over the amount of time you spend playing computer games
- By getting your mum to ask

How to Be Cool on A Hen Night

The answer that most people would give is 'stay in'. That's because of the recent explosion in hen nights and the attendant industries that have grown up around them. There are now companies that specialise in booking hen and stag nights. And so most of us are now sick of the faith-in-humanity-crushing sight of a group of drunk women shrieking their way through a piss and puke-soaked town centre with Deely Bopper dicks on their heads and matching T-shirts emblazoned with the name of the hen and the slogan 'Any Cock'll Do!' It really does make you think that maybe global warming is the planet's way of wiping us out, and not before time.

The cool way to have a hen night, and the same goes for a stag night, is to make it a *night*. Too many people these days have a weekend, often involving flights, car rental and accommodation charges. We're already shelling out hundreds for the wedding, and now we've got to spend another wodge of cash traipsing round third-rate night clubs while you try to get off with random strangers and drunkenly agonise over whether you're making the right choice marrying someone you've already been living with for five years. A total waste of everyone's time.

Instead, why not just organise drinks and a nice meal with your oldest friends. Most hen nights are spiritually degrading, so already a simple night like that is leagues ahead in terms of its relative coolness. As long as you avoid the following activities, you're in the clear:

- Sex on bins, benches, car bonnets, toilets and turntables of a DJ booth

- Any kind of headgear, feather boas and, above all, matching T-shirts. Unless you want people to cast their eyes downwards and mutter prayers of forgiveness as you enter a room
- Making innuendoes and passes at waiters. They don't want to have sex with you. They just want to go home
- The ruining of a comedy evening through incessant drunken babble of supreme irrelevance to the surrounding audience and performers

How to Be Cool On a Stag Night

As I've said, make it a night. Don't bankrupt your friends and use up their weekend with an extravagant farewell to the boys. Time was a stag night was the groom's friends giving him a send-off before he embarks on a new life with his bride. But nowadays it's a reluctant man haemorrhaging his savings on rings and honeymoons for a woman he's already semi-committed to but is sticking with because he can't see himself doing any better in the foreseeable future. So make it a muted evening down the pub. Not that paint-balling and go-carting aren't fun, it's just that stag nights are usually fairly disparate groups made up of the following people:

- Loudmouth beer-guzzler who thinks that being the life and soul involves singing 'I'm Too Sexy' with an ice bucket on his head
- Anal retentive organisation freak who keeps moving everyone on so they can stick to the timetable of planned events
- Some poor sod who doesn't know anyone, possibly the bride's brother or a cousin of the groom
- Old school friend of the groom he hasn't seen for years and who, in the intervening period, has developed some fairly racist views
- Friend of the groom who thinks he's selling out by tying the knot. Usually single himself, resents the bride and has a possible sublimated homosexual crush on the groom
- Married man with kids who hasn't been let out in years and lobbies strongly for a strip club
- Someone who keeps trying to instigate a whip-round to pay the stripper to provide 'extras'

It's a total powder keg, and is best kept in a contained environment, i.e. one or two locations and under a finite pre-determined period, e.g. an evening. Any deviation from this can lead to profound regret.

How to Be Cool as a Groom

The main thing to do is to enter into it with a willing heart. That means you can't say the following out loud, no matter how strongly their sentiments burn inside you, or how subtly you think you're making your point:

- 'Do we need flowers in the church?'
- 'I'm sure it's a beautiful dress, but that is quite a lot of money and you are only going to wear it once . . .'
- 'It's not that I don't want them to come, it's just I've never really clicked with him/her . . .'
- 'There are a lot of good quality sparkling wines these days that taste as good as champagne for a fraction of the price!'
- 'We could pay £500 for a string quartet. Or, we could pay £15 for a Vivaldi CD'
- 'This is getting out of hand. My mate can take the photos.'
- 'A horse-drawn carriage is romantic, but what if one of the horses breaks down? I don't know, maybe it loses a shoe? My point is you know where you are with Addison Lee . . .'
- 'I've always liked those caterpillar cakes from Marks and Spencers'
- 'An iPod and a shuffle button are all the DJ we need'

If you want to be cool to her friends and family and most importantly to her, then hand over your bank details and smile through it. Just don't think 'We could have bought a Porsche instead . . .', you'll start crying. Although, actually all the women will find that really cool if you cry on your wedding day, so keep that thought. Here are some other things you could have spent at the money that will prompt a sob:

- Five holidays
- An extension
- A new kitchen
- A home cinema system
- A year off

No matter how tempting it is, it is uncool when accepting an award or accolade to say 'Eat my ass losers!'

How to Be Cool as a Bride

An easy rule of thumb is to ask yourself if your wedding is anything like Jordan's. If it is, stop now. Her wedding was like a nightmarish cross between Willy Wonka and *East-*

Enders. She also swore during her speech – classy. And Peter Andre sweated like, well like a man just about to marry Jordan. Also, don't do anything that has a hint of the Beckhams' wedding. Or indeed any other footballer or mime puppet's wedding. The no-nos in terms of cool are:

- Pumpkin coaches
- Matching bride and groom suits
- The presence of Jodie Marsh, Paul Danan or anyone from *Big Brother*
- Strippers
- Black Lace covers band

How to Be Cool as a Best Man

This is a lot of pressure. You've have to be witty and charming, a little bit cheeky, and then compliment everyone on a great day and what a lovely couple they are. Tricky if a week before you watched him drink champagne from a stripper's cleavage, or you've been having an affair with her.

There're all sorts of duties you're supposed to undertake, organisational stuff and so forth. But the bit that everyone cares about and gets to see is the speech. So

- Don't go too blue. There are kids and grandparents in the room. Use code. I once referred to the groom's well-known love of pornography as his 'well-known love of jazz. Particularly hardcore Eastern European jazz'. His friends had a laugh, everyone else thought he was a sophisticated jazz lover. Everybody wins.

- If it's there, try to hide your contempt for the bride. Don't make jokes about her 'punching above her weight'. In fact, no references to weight at all.
- No matter how amusing the anecdote, or how much you think it paints the groom in a good light, do not mention any ex-girlfriends.

How to Be Cool as the Bride and Groom

This mainly concerns the first dance. Most couples now train for months to do a proper first dance. This can be really cool, especially if everyone has one of you (usually the groom) down as a total clodhopper. Whilst the choice of song for first dance is down to the individual couple, it is best to avoid the songs listed below if you want to impress everyone with how cool you are as newlyweds.

- 'Animal Fuck Like A Beast', W.A.S.P.
- 'The Revealing Science Of God', Yes (full 20-minute version)
- 'In A Big Country', Big Country

- 'Crockett's Theme', Jan Hammer
- 'The Final Countdown', Europe
- 'Bond Smells A Rat', soundtrack to *Moonraker*
- 'The Birdy Song', The Tweets
- 'Giving The Dog A Bone', AC/DC
- 'Main Titles', soundtrack to *Where Eagles Dare*
- *Archangel*, Michael Gambon reads the audiobook of Robert Harris's novel
- Anything by the Spice Girls

How to Be Cool on Honeymoon

The coolness here really comes down to destination rather than how you behave. Although it's not cool if your behaviour involves sleeping with other people. At least give that till you're back in your own country. Try and avoid:

- Separate destinations. This sends out a very worrying signal
- Groom in first class, bride in economy. Very uncool
- Trek across Siberian tundra
- Tour of WW2 battlefields (unlikely to excite bride)
- Blackpool
- Location tour of the *Terminator* movies

How to Be Cool When Dumping People

There is just no way of doing this and being cool. The last way the dumpee is ever going to spin it to their friends is 'They dumped me, but they were really cool about it.' You shouldn't come across as cool, unless they deserve it. The following are acceptable reasons to need to dump someone:

- They steal money off you for drugs
- The only reason they haven't slept with all of your friends is that one of them is in a coma
- You catch them assembling a dirty bomb in your lounge

And there are uncool reasons to dump someone:

- A general feeling that you could do better
- Time spent with them is cutting into the time you like to spend paying for sex
- You've got a bet with a friend that you can sleep with a new person every day for a month
- They wouldn't let you have a potty by the bed
- They didn't agree with you that *Speed 2: Cruise Control* is the best film ever made
- They tried to hem you in by asking what you were doing at Christmas

But if it's a case of things just not clicking, let them down gently. Take them to dinner and explain how you're not good enough for them, you have to let them go so they can find a lover worthy of them.

How to Be Cool When You've Been Dumped

We've all been there, you're at your lowest ebb – the person you thought you were going to spend the rest of your life with has told you they never want to see you again. At first you can't even admit it to your friends and family, it's too painful. It's as though saying it out loud makes it true, and if you keep it to yourself, maybe it didn't happen, or maybe they'll change their mind. Well, here's how to deal with it with dignity. The temptation is to pay someone unbelievably hot to pretend to be your new partner and to tell everyone you left your former partner because of their continuing addiction to Internet porn and heroin. No, you have to take it on the chin. They don't want to be with you. What are you going to do? Beg? Stalk them? Deeply uncool reactions. You've got to make them think it's their loss. And you do that by being reasonable and understanding. This will unnerve them – why is this person reacting with such equilibrium? I'm supposed to be breaking their heart. No one can live without me! Carry on the 'no big deal' act as best you can. Either suggest or agree that you remain friends and are adult about this. And then never be available if they call. And make sure you have some cool excuses. No 'I'm catching up on sleep, work's a nightmare.' It's got to be:

- A date
- A singles party organised by a hot friend they know
- A film premier
- A sold-out must-see gig

Above all, try to avoid the following uncool reactions:

- Spreading a rumour they've got Aids
- Writing 'I do it for biscuits' and their phone number on toilet doors
- Posting them all the photos you have of the two of you together in a box with a dead rat
- Reporting them as suspects every time there's a murder hunt in your area
- Telling them you get more emotional support from the sex workers you now regularly visit

In the 21st century, with all the advantages of modern tailoring, there is simply no need to wear braces

How to Be Cool When Your Friends Have a Baby

This can stir up a lot of emotions, especially if you are not yet a parent, or are single. You can feel left behind, or that they're moving ahead too fast. But control your feelings. If you're a male friend, it's not cool to do any of the following:

- Bitch and moan about how the father has sold out
- Talk about how the mother will never get her figure back
- Talk about how you'll see them when it's time to buy the kid its first pint, which you put at thirteen

If you're a female friend, it's definitely uncool to:

- Sob uncontrollably about how you'll never be a mother
- Hit on the father
- Steal the baby

In the eyes of the kid, what's going to be cooler than having a friend of their parents dote on them? You get to be there for all the fun parts, and don't have to deal with any of the sleepless nights, nappy changing and temper tantrums that pepper parenting. And it's not just the kid who'll think you're cool! If you're a single man, demonstrating your love of children is one of the coolest things you can do in front of women. It doesn't matter how old or young you are, that's always going to get you points. If you're a single woman, it's slightly different. Great if the man you're after wants to settle down; he'll see you as a good deal. Not so good if your prospective boyfriend wants a few more years of lie-ins and spontaneous social activity. Your doting on someone else's child will scare the life out of him. To him you're just a big literal mantrap. He'll leave you citing reasons like 'You're too good for me' and 'I'm just not in that place right now'. So don't do any doting in front of him till you catch him wandering doe-eyed into the Baby section in Gap, or crying at the end of *Three Men And A Baby*, at which point you'll know the time is right. Although, actually, if he cries at the end of *Three Men And A Baby*, you might want to get him checked out by a mental-healthcare professional. Especially if, in between sobs, he's saying 'Leonard Nimoy . . . never got the credit he deserved . . . as a director . . . people just think he's Spock . . . but he's so much more than that . . .'

RELATIONSHIP
COOLOMETER TEST

1 Your partner asks you to attend the funeral of a relative. Do you

a) Say 'I don't know, what music will they play?'

b) Hide behind the nearest piece of furniture shrieking 'bums, tits and willies' in a high-pitched voice

c) Offer your support and make all the travel arrangements

d) Ask 'Were they a square or a cat? I don't dig no squares, but I'll wave off a cat to the sky disco'

2 You are walking in a park with your partner when a dog starts jumping up on you. Do you

a) Grab the dog's paws and rip it apart at the sternum, then say to the horrified onlookers 'Any one of you would have done the same!'

b) Cup the dog's balls and say 'Let me milk him'

c) Laugh along until its owner gets it under control

d) Say 'Even animals want a piece of Me Pie!'

3 **Someone you fancy at a party asks you what you do for a living. Do you**

a) Reply 'Kill people who ask too many questions' then leave via the nearest window

b) Say 'If I answer that it is on the understanding that I have absolutely no interest in asking you the same question. Fuck?'

c) Answer the question with brevity and charm before focussing on them

d) Say 'What do I do for a living? How about who I do for a living?' Then grab their genital region and whisper 'Tonight is about tonight'

4 **Your partner's parents ask you when you think you'll start a family. Do you**

e) Hide under the nearest table claiming to be a mole

f) Say 'When I meet someone worthy of my DNA'

g) Reply that you've haven't really thought about it yet, but they'll be the first to know

h) Say 'No time like the present' and start trying to dry-hump your partner's leg

5 **Your new partner tells you they regularly take part in phone votes for TV talent shows. Do you**

a) Make love to them in a Simon Cowell face mask

b) Leave them without saying a word

c) Remark how you don't really watch them but that's more a time issue and they seem like great fun

d) Say 'The only *X Factor* I care about is screwing my exes after they've met me to tell me they're engaged'

If you answered mainly 'a', on the positive side, you will keep the 'ready-meal-for-one' market alive for years to come.

If you answered mainly 'b', your name is on everyone's lips! But mainly when the topic turns to 'worst date you've ever been on'.

If you answered mainly 'c', congratulations, you are a cool partner! Don't blow it by doing the voice of Popeye when you make love.

If you answered mainly 'd', put it this way, the only chat-up line that is ever going to work for you is a post-apocalypse 'Please. The survival of the human race depends on it.'

Chapter 9

HOW TO REGAIN YOUR COOL

All of us, on occasion, get knocked off balance – you come back from the toilet with your shirt poking through your flies, or accidentally spit at someone while you're talking to them. Here's how to get through it without the need to fake your own death.

How to Be Cool When You Bump Into Someone Who Doesn't Remember You

It seems everyone is cursed with at least one individual – it may be a work colleague, it may be the spouse of a friend – who never, ever remembers who you are. Less common, but it still happens, is bumping into people from school or university who clearly have no idea who you are. How do you deal with this in a cool manner, when what they are clearly saying is 'You are an unmemorable blank of a person, whom I erase from my brain as soon as you leave my field of vision'? It could be that they do it on purpose as part of a status game, it could be that they have genuine problems with recollection. Either way, they deserve your pity. Don't let their absent-mindedness, or purposeful rudeness, put you on the back foot. Just shake hands, fix them in the eye, and proffer one of the following explanations:

- 'I looked very different last time you saw me. I'd just got back from a North African desert trek'
- 'Honestly, it's not a problem. I forgot Kevin Spacey's name the other week, he gave me such a look!'

How to Be Cool When You've Accidentally Sprayed Water on Your Crotch at the Sink in a Restaurant

This has happened to the best of us. You're using an unfamiliar tap in a sink best described as an 'accelerator'. The result – worst-case scenario is you look like you've wet yourself, best-case scenario is you look like you've sprayed water all over yourself. Now, maintaining your cool depends on who you're with. If you're with an old friend or partner of some time, you can probably laugh about it. If it's a first date or a business meeting, it gives a very, very bad impression. Basically, you're either incontinent or extremely clumsy. Your options are few and desperate:

- You can soak the rest of your trousers or skirt and hope the uniformity of colour means they don't look closer to see you're sopping wet

- You can remove the clothing on your lower torso and replace them with a patchwork of paper towels, which you then claim you've been wearing all the time
- You can create another spillage as a diversionary tactic, i.e. knock a glass of wine in one of your fellow diner's laps
- You can climb out of a window and claim you were the victim of a kidnapping/bout of amnesia, etc.

For coolness, I suggest you go with a big lie. One of the following:

- You came across someone fainting in the toilet, or being violently sick, and had to clean them up and help them on their way
- The chef begged you to come and help strain some vegetables; they were out of aprons, but it had to be done quick as there's a reviewer in
- You gamely stood in the way of a violent husband throwing water at his wife

How to Be Cool When a Woman Knows You've Been Staring at Her Breasts

All men stare at women's breasts, and all women know that men stare at their breasts. But there's a tacit agreement that, as long as it isn't too obvious, both parties don't mind. However, if eye contact is made as a man raises his eyes from breast to face, he's in trouble. He's gone from casting a subtle and admiring eye to being a disgusting lech. How to get round this and maintain your cool equilibrium? There's no point in denying it – 'I wasn't staring at your breasts' is not going to put you back on track. The best way to do it is to launch into an important point so that she will think you weren't staring at her breasts, your eyes were locked there in an unseeing introspective haze as you grappled with a deeply serious issue. Choose from the following and you'll be fine:

- 'Sorry, I was miles away. Just wondering how that child I'm sponsoring is doing'
- 'How the hell does America get away with its outrageous foreign policy?'
- 'Forgive me, I suddenly thought I was supposed to be at that Amnesty meeting, but that's next week'
- 'Do you think, if Shakespeare was alive today, he'd be writing for TV or film?'
- 'So many religions . . . so much hate'

210

> **COOL TAKEWAYS**
> Indian, Thai, Japanese
> **UNCOOL TAKEWAYS**
> Hot dogs from a stand, contents of neighbour's
> recycling bins, pick'n'mix

How to Be Cool When You Make a Pass at a Party and Are Knocked Back

A friend once said to me that, if someone knocks you back, it's no worse than not liking a particular dish of food, or trying on a T-shirt that is the wrong fit. There's no shame on anyone's part, it just didn't work out. True enough. Except ordering badly in a restaurant or getting the wrong size clothing doesn't make you want to fight back tears and snarl 'You just missed the best night of your life, now crawl on back to Loserville, I hear you've bought up most of the property there. Hell, you're Mayor of Loserville!' If it does, then this book probably isn't going to sort out your problems. Cool requires composure, dignity. That isn't conveyed by you screaming 'Fine, I didn't want herpes anyway!' at someone who doesn't want to sleep with you. If it's a pass that you can both agree to ignore, i.e. it wasn't too blatant, then fine, just gear-change into a neutral topic of conversation and then try to manoeuvre your way out of there as soon as possible. If, however, you feel really exposed by the pass and you both know what you've just done, then time for some expert advice.

The main thing is you have to either leave them immediately, or talk for a long time. There can be no 'idle chat for five minutes-oh look over there-I really must . . . is that the time?-nice to meet you'. That's too obvious and awkward and uncool. You have to be mature and composed. This is for two reasons:

1 They might not fancy you, or might already be in a relationship, but they may introduce you to a single friend
2 You might be able to pull it round

So, you either say 'Well, you can't blame me for trying, you're the most attractive person here, so I thought I'd get in early. Sorry if I've embarrassed you. I'm going to go over there now, maybe later we can bump into each other, pretend that didn't just happen and chat as friends?', which will intrigue them. You've given them a compliment and left. It's like you didn't want anything back! How cool is that? What confidence and poise. Or, say the first bit, but hang around talking, though with no hint of flirtatious or sexual content. Again, you'll look cool because you've flagged your intentions, but then are completely respecting the boundaries they've set. This is much, much cooler than trying too hard by saying things like:

- 'You sure? Last chance . . . fine. Screw you!'
- 'Go on, you might like it. I won't tell anyone!'
- 'You are a walled medieval city, and I am an army camped outside your gates. An army, with a siege engine!'
- 'Regret is a dish that you, my friend, will choke on.'
- 'Everyone has their price . . .'

How to Be Cool When You've Run for a Train or Bus and Missed It

How cool is it to run and leap on a moving vehicle? Very. But we all know how uncool it is to miss it, even by a matter of seconds. Everyone around you knows you were running for a reason, and that you weren't fast or nimble enough to make it. You're left sweating and hyperventilating, like Eamonn Holmes trying to do up his shoelaces. Well, the cool thing to do, if you can, is not to slow down, just keep running as though you weren't even going for the bus; you're just a person in a hurry. Fine for a bus, I hear you say, but not for a train. You can't exactly start running along the track. There are a couple of options:

- Run alongside it for as long as you can, pointing down and mouthing the word 'bomb' . . . This will momentarily wipe the smiles off the faces of those people laughing at your tardy efforts to hop on board. Of course, if there is a bomb, you will be the target in a worldwide manhunt. Maybe it's better to try to give an impression of the magnitude of you missing that train. Other people might be on it for a jaunt, something to do, it gets them out of the house and away from daytime quizzes and loan adverts filled with people who see McDonalds as a treat, but goddamn it, you had to be on it! Exclaim something like:

1. 'Damn it! I'll have to get the chopper to pick me up!'
2. 'Cut me a break! I'm just trying to deliver an antidote to some sick kids!'
3. 'Damn it! They don't call him "The Fox" for nothing! Yet again he slips away!'

How to Be Cool When You've Tripped in the Street

Now this happens to us all, a trip for no discernible reason. What to do? There's no one to blame but you. Cool people don't trip, they don't falter: they just keep gliding on with ineffable poise. The standard response is to turn the trip into the start of a run that continues until you're out of sight of all those who saw you make the original trip. Or to turn it into a downward movement as though you need to check something on your shoe. Those are probably your best options. You certainly can't:

- Burst into tears
- Start hitting the pavement with your shoe
- Try to kick anyone who sniggered at you

> Never display a framed photo of Margaret Thatcher

How to Be Cool When Your Stash of Pornography is Discovered

In a digital age, a stash may soon be no more. We've already seen the decline of the magazine. No longer do teenagers have the feral joy of discovering a magazine in the woods. These days it's all on tap via the Internet. But DVDs still do a roaring trade. These can't be filed in with your other films, so they have to be hidden in a stash. Retaining your coolness on its discovery depends on two things. Who caught you, and how much you have. If your parents have caught you, then that's just agony, unless you have the kind of liberal parents who have always been open about such matters. Then the only coolness to be had from that situation is telling your friends that your parents caught you, and they didn't mind. But don't, under any circumstances, lie about that. If your parents smashed them up with a hammer, it's not going to ease the tension if, the next time your friends come round, they say 'I wish my parents were like you and bought me porn!' If you're a woman and your partner has found your porn, relax! As far as your boyfriend is concerned, trust me, you just hit the cool jackpot. You could not be cooler in his eyes. That's like finding out that drinking cures cancer. But if you're a man and your partner has found your porn, you have to tread very, very carefully indeed. Now, whilst many women secretly admit to finding porn a turn-on, there are some things they will definitely find uncool:

- A massive collection. It's not cool if it looks like you're running a shop
- Titles featuring certain acts they have been unwilling to perform, or that, whilst not illegal, are definitely not right
- Films featuring porn stars who look unnervingly like one of your ex-girlfriends or a friend/sister/female relative of your partner
- Films of a sexuality different to your own

How to Be Cool When You're Sweating Uncontrollably

This can just happen. Maybe you rushed to get somewhere, or you've passed through some extremes of temperature: there could be a variety of reasons. But one thing's for sure, it doesn't look good. People associate sweating with the following things:

- Nervousness
- Unfitness
- Body odour

So you have to dispel these associations and regain your cool both literally and figuratively. First remove excess layers of clothing and drink something cold. Not in a panicked 'Oh God help me here, I'm drowning in my own skin-secreted waste products!' kind of way. In a measured and calm way. Then say things like:

- 'That's better. Sorry about that, I've come straight from marathon training'
- 'Malaria. Had a touch ever since the tropics'
- 'Sorry, I've found that Antarctic trek has shot my internal thermostat to pieces. But it was worth it for the sunsets. The light on a iceberg is one of the purest refractions of energy in the special effects lab we call the earth'

All of those give reasons, and paint you as sensitive, widely travelled and aware of the limitations of the human body, even as you strive against them.

How to Be Cool When Waking Up In Public with Dribble on Your Shoulder

There's no getting away from the fact that this looks bad. We've all fallen asleep on public transport, and some of us have woken up with drool down our chin and on our clothes. Now you might be lucky, people might not notice. If so, then simply wipe your chin as subtly as you can and rearrange your body into the position of someone who looks like they can hold a conversation without running to the toilet. But if you have been spotted, you may as well know that people now think you are one of three things:

1 A drunk
2 A tramp
3 A drunk tramp

You have to counteract this image. Give them a reason to think you're cool. There is a romance around drunks; you could make out you've just been to a fabulous party by saying 'J-Lo, no!' or 'Clooney, you dog!' as you come round.

Or you could convey that your current state of disorientation is due to overwork for a cool reason. Don't say 'Damn sales figures had me up all night. It's not my fault. People just aren't buying goddamn toasters right now!' Give it a 'Sorry. Fifty hours on my feet in the ER kind of takes it out of me. If it's any consolation, that bus-load of kids will make it to that Harry Potter film. A later showing than they wanted, but they'll make it.' Or go for it, pretend you're a top British agent who's survived a near-fatal poisoning – 'Did you see anyone put anything in my coffee? I've got to get to the PM before the mole!'

How to Be Cool When You Tread in Dog Mess or Sick

As the streets of our cities increasingly resemble the floors of a prison during a protest, this is, sadly, a regular occurrence. If you're on your own, it's not too bad: it's inconvenient, but you can scrape it off. If you're in company, it's difficult to keep your coolness: just deal with it as quickly and as inconspicuously as you can. If you've slid on it, fallen over and got it all up your back, then the coolest thing to do is to say you'll catch them up in a bit and then go and buy a complete new outfit on the spot. And go way beyond your price range so they think 'Wow, that's the kind of stuff they grab in a hurry!' After, take it back and swap it for something cheaper. Please remember that, although one of the aspects of cool I've stressed is being unfazed and going with the flow, that does not apply here. Do not, under any circumstances, if you have faeces or vomit on your clothes, shrug it off and say 'Who cares, let's eat!'

How to Be Cool When You're Soundly Beaten at a Computer Game by Someone a Quarter of Your Age

I can tell you right now that it's uncool to lose it or be rattled in anyway. No matter how tempting it is to throw the controller at the wall and shout 'Enough of this shit! How much money do you make in a year? Can you drive a car? How many people have you slept with?' it won't help, and in the case of the last question, they may well trump your score if the current surveys on the sexual mores of Britain's youth are to be believed.

Now, they will be laughing at you, there's no doubt about it. But you have to take it on the chin with good grace. Flatter them, make them feel cool about how skilled they are – kids today, etc., such a wide range of skills shown. People knock computer games but, my, how good their hand-eye co-ordination is, how quick their reflexes are. Spin that out. Then go home, buy a console of your own, practise every hour that God sends you, then casually suggest a rematch when you next see them, and beat them like a Viking raiding a village of peace-loving Pygmies.

How to Be Cool When You Beat Someone a Quarter of Your Age at a Computer Game

When you do win the rematch, though, don't end it with 'There you go, you piece of shit! Who's the daddy now! You done got beat! How's that feel! How's it feel to be my bitch?!' Likewise ignore any suggestions they might make that you might have been training for this for months. Just shrug it off and say 'I guess last time must have been an off day.'

REGAINING YOUR COOL
COOLOMETER TEST

1 You trip up in the street and a small child laughs at you. Do you

a) Tell the child that Father Christmas will kill his parents

b) Start slapping the pavement crying 'Who's the pussy now?!'

c) Laugh it off and carry on your way

d) Say to the kid 'This shiny pound says that never happened' and throw it at their head

2 You accidentally break wind at a social event. Do you

a) Grab the person next to you by the throat and scream 'Why are you trying to poison me? Your butt stinks of death!'

b) Say 'I normally fart when I'm horny. But you, you make me want to shit'

c) Slowly move everyone away from the affected area

d) Say 'Get me a match, I'm ready for lift off!'

3 You offer to buy a stranger a drink. They decline the offer. Do you

a) Make a citizen's arrest declaiming 'No, I won't plant a bomb as part of your Holy War!'

b) Say 'What about crisps then? Nuts? Fags? Condoms? WHAT DO YOU WANT FROM ME?'

c) Say 'Well, you can't blame me for trying' and leave them alone

d) Say 'The regret I feel at your rejection is nothing compared to the regret you'd feel waking up next to me . . . no hang on, other way round. Anyway, I gotta split. The stench of desperation is making me retch.'

4 A group of menacing kids are gathered on the pavement in front of your flat. Do you

a) Dance up to them singing 'I'm a dirty paedo! I'm a dirty paedo!'

b) Book into a hotel and call the police for an escort

c) Walk calmly through them avoiding eye contact

d) Walk calmly through them, then stop to say 'Got any smokes? You cats would dig the new Santana album. He buzzing like a bee on Lucozade. Ouch!'

5 You tread in dog shit on a date. Do you

a) Pretend to eat it, saying 'Me no like shitty shoe!'
b) Take off your shoe and wipe it on your date's back crying 'You wouldn't find it disgusting if you loved me!'
c) Scrape it off
d) Take off your shoes and throw them in a bin because 'In my book, shitty = history'

If you answered mainly 'a', ouch, you've tripped on a downward slope and your fat belly is greased.

If you answered mainly 'b', just give up now. You leak cool like an incontinent man at a pissing contest.

If you answered mainly 'c', good work, if you lose it, you can get it back. Unlike Jude Law and his hairline.

If you answered mainly 'd', you're the cool equivalent of *Indiana Jones and the Kingdom of the Crystal Skull*: i.e. you're fine in principal but are actually a massive shit.

It's cool to surprise someone with the fact you can speak French or Japanese. Not so cool with Klingon

Chapter 10
COOL THROUGH THE AGES

What's cool when you're six (lego, dressing up) isn't the same as what's cool when you're sixty (buying a lawnmower you can drive). This will show you what to do when.

How to Be Cool as a Teenager

DO – to be cool within your peer group, it seems you must be volatile, monosyllabic, aggressive, the carrier of three of the major STDs, have no awareness of any cultural or historical figures before 1989 and no ambitions beyond thieving and raping your way to an ineffective control order that merely increases your coolness in the eyes of your idiotic maggot-like cohorts.

DON'T – study, or in anyway contribute to the well-being of those around you or the wider society.

How to Be Cool in Your Twenties

DO – Be your own person! You can't be tied down to society's definition of success, this is your last chance to travel, meet new people and get your hair braided. Get a gay friend! Or maybe a tattoo! Have sex with someone in a club toilet! Then get your parents to pay off your debts before you start a proper career!

DON'T – Work in the City, you might think you're cool, but actually you're a c**t.

How to Be Cool in Your Thirties

DO – OK, time to get serious. Now, it's all right to buy property and commit to a relationship. It's not selling out, it's sensible. Actually, it's cool; it shows maturity and responsibility.

DON'T – Panic and sink all your money into your play about Bob Marley and Buddy Holly sharing a bedsit with George Best.

How to Be Cool in Your Forties

DO – Listen up, you really have to pack away that Play-Station. It was cool in your thirties, now it's getting a little creepy. You can still be cool in your own way – develop a knowledge of wine or malt whiskies, buy a Merc or a BMW. If you really need a cool top-up, you could go to a gig by that year's Kaiser Chiefs.

DON'T – under any circumstances decide this is the time to get a tattoo, piercing, mistress, toy boy, facelift, paunch or pay for a threesome.

How to Be Cool in Your Fifties

DO – You're through to the other side now. You don't have to care, and that makes you cool. No one expects you to be cool, so anything you do that's even vaguely cool gets you double points. Use the word 'shit' in front of teenagers. Go on a march. Hand out leaflets against a phone mast at your local farmers' market.
DON'T – Join UKIP.

How to Be Cool as a Pensioner

DO – Take an interest in new books, films and technology.
DON'T – Accuse your neighbours of being sleeper terrorist agents.

COOL JOBS TO ASPIRE TO AS A KID
Astronaut, film star, rock star, pioneering scientist
UNCOOL JOBS TO ASPIRE TO AS A KID
Chicken sexer, bare-knuckle boxing promoter, fake dog turd designer, manager of the Krispy Kreme Donut store at Heathrow Terminal 4

COOL THROUGH
THE AGES COOLOMETER TEST

1 **It's your twenty-first birthday party. Do you**

a) Neck twenty-one shots of absinthe and proclaim yourself
the returning Christ

b) Demand that your friends write twenty-one poems with
twenty-one lines and twenty-one syllables per line about
all your achievements

c) Have a party

d) Get drunk, shout about how Alexander the Great had
conquered many lands by the time he was your age,
then stagger off to invade Greece

2 **You're fifteen and it's a Saturday. Do you**

a) Get drunk and set fire to things

b) Get high and throw things at people

c) Hang out with your friends

d) Slouch menacingly on benches in a local shopping
centre boasting about how you're going to be rich like
that guy in *Scarface*

3 You're about to turn thirty. Do you

a) Panic you haven't slept with enough people and set about rectifying it with the use of bribes, adverts and begging

b) Say to everyone you meet 'Why are you so fucking happy? I'm as good as dead!'

c) Organise a celebratory event with friends and family

d) Walk out of your job and form a punk band

4 You receive your first state pension. Do you

a) Donate it to 'Migration Watch'

b) Embarrass yourself by entering a beatbox competition

c) Feel slightly underwhelmed at the paltry amount

d) Blow it on the dogs then claim you were mugged by a 'foreign chappy'

5 You're in your forties and you worry your marriage has turned stale. Do you

a) Start graffiti tagging in your street and when questioned blame it on sexual rejection from your spouse
b) Say to younger couples 'Be warned, the fucky-fucky will stop and you will be left questioning why you even bother to draw breath'
c) Set aside more time to spend with your spouse
d) Work your way through all the contact mag listings in your area

If you answered mainly 'a', the bad news – you're never going to be cool. The good news – you can stop washing and can start patting the backsides of strangers.

If you answered mainly 'b', you and cool have as much of a future as a Steven Seagal guide to better love-making.

If you answered mainly 'c', you'll be cool until you die. But when the time comes to put your effects in order, you *must* destroy that box under your bed.

If you answered mainly 'd', wow, a c-word will come up a lot at your funeral, but it won't be 'cool'.

Chapter 11

HOW TO LAUNCH YOUR COOL ON THE WORLD

After reading this book, you may want to go through a bit of a cool makeover. And there are various ways you can do this. The key thing is to make it gradual. Cool should flow from within, it shouldn't appear as though you've read a book and started dressing like a biker from the future. Here are some other things to avoid:

- Wacky business cards. They went out with Timmy Mallett
- A 'Cool' coming out party

One way to do it is to have a MySpace page. Or a page on one of the other social networking sites. If you don't know which one is for you, as far as I can tell they can best be summed up as follows:

- MySpace – the daddy of them all. From an emo-obsessed teenager to the President of the United States, everybody's got a page.
- Bebo – this is the Betamax to the VHS of MySpace. I don't mean it's a superior product and less aggressively marketed, but it's clearly going to be overwhelmed at some point.

- **Facebook – this is MySpace for young urban professionals. I hesitate to think of how many work hours in white-collar work environments were lost to this in the last twelve months.**

MySpace is like one big advert. People use it for different things – dating, promoting their band, making themselves feel more important in the scheme of things than they are. It's also a chance for you to remake yourself in your own chosen image. It can be a tightrope act, though. As ever there's a fine line between 'cool' and 'wanker'.

> As a man, never tuck your trousers into your boots

PHOTO

It goes without saying that this is important. It's your visual signature, it sets the tone for the entire page. You need to think about the subtle messages and subtexts you are sending out. For instance

- Wacky – I am not wacky
- Moody – I fancy myself. Now this is OK if you're genuinely hot, but if it's just a good photo that seems

out of place amongst the rest on your photo page, you're done for

- Baby pic – only of interest to those who already know you, you're not looking to spread your wings of cool

HEADLINE

This is the blurb that appears next to your photo. It's the first thing people see. Here are some of the standard options and what they convey:

- Bob Dylan quote – intense and arty
- Quote from *The Goonies* – I was born in the early 80s
- Something that makes no sense – I haven't really thought about this

BACKGROUNDS

Again, the overall visual impression reflects your personality. The main thing is don't choose something that takes an age to load up. People lose patience. And be aware of the signals you are sending out, e.g.

- Large airbrushed picture of man fighting dragon – I have a sex dungeon
- Moving static – I am grudgingly entering my thirties and worry that my book about the sale of memories in a future infotainment state may not see the light of day

- Bunnies blowing heart-shaped kisses – I have developmental problems

SONG

You can't go wrong with something classic and upbeat. You *can* go wrong, though, it you try too hard to be cool. Something wilfully obscure or atonal will turn people off. Ironic is fine, you could go with 'Frankie' by Sister Sledge. Just don't have a long blog entry about how it's the best song ever and anyone who can't see it deserves to be put to the sword.

INTERESTS

As an overall note, keep it short and to the point. List the films you like, not every film in the '1000 Great Films You've Never Heard Of' *Observer* supplement. If you were at a social function and someone asked your interests, you wouldn't talk till you fainted from hunger, so don't do it on the net. After a while, it's like watching someone masturbating – you think it's going to be fun and a useful anecdote, but it's just awkward and you want them to finish, but in another room.

MUSIC

Now there's no doubt that it's cool to like obscure music. It shows a level of knowledge beyond the person on the street; it's exotic and shows a high level of individuality. Choose a few of the following fictional bands to top up your cool. But for Christ's sake, don't make every band obscure: it's impenetrable to read.

- The Tins
- Pappy's Randy Monkey
- Justin Lamanza
- Diavolo Da Vinci
- Death Hogs
- Slitmuncher
- The Electric Lawnmowers
- King Mustapha Wembayo
- The Flying Travoltas
- Dirty Dickie's Dumphouse
- Boilerplate
- Me Like Fatties
- The Coils
- Ribbed For Pleasure
- The Cock Rings
- The Dandy Highwaymen
- MC8X2
- Big Bill's Ill In Bed
- Dirty Vicars

- PMT
- Fuckrage
- Rough Fair Trade

Names not to include, as they are 'Evaporators of Cool':

- Chaka Demus and Pliers
- Owen Paul
- Haddaway
- 5ive
- Culture Beat
- Another Level
- K–Fed
- 2 Unlimited
- Snap
- The London Boys

MOVIES

Same as music, a bunch of classics peppered with a few no one's heard of. It says 'I support my local independent cinema and will buy their overpriced flapjacks and put up with their crappy sound. But I'm not averse to shoving lumps of salty fat down my mouth in a multiplex watching Jason Statham stamp on a guy's balls whilst failing to sustain an American accent.' Pick some of these:

- *How To Honour Your Father And Mother*
- *Faria's Tears*
- *FTC (Fuck The Corporations)*
- *The Oceans Of My Brain*
- *Van Gogh's Cat*
- *On A Gay Day You Can See Forever*
- *Ten Things I Never Did Before I Died*
- *God's Jukebox*
- *Home Is A Hard Drive*
- *Dance Virgins*
- *Sex Medicine*
- *Ghosts Of Genghis Khan*
- *Homeopathia*
- *Painting Strawberries*
- *A Year In The Day Of A Shanty Town*

Films everyone lists on MySpace that are cool:

- *Goodfellas*
- *Lord Of The Rings*
- *Star Wars* (original trilogy NOT prequels)
- *LA Confidential*
- *Gladiator*

Films no one should ever list on MySpace, even when trying to be ironically cool:

- *Turner and Hooch*
- *K9*
- all other 'cop-dog-buddy movies'
- *Rancid Aluminium* (officially the worst film ever, an ironic watch will still make you want to hurt something)

BOOKS

You're always going to look cool listing anything by Don Delillo, Martin Amis, Salman Rushdie and Umberto Eco. Chuck in some classics – Dickens, Eliot, Melville – and you're nearly home and dry. All you need are a couple of obscure titles so people feel they need to know you. Try these:

- *The Memory of Snails*
- *The Tea-Leaf Reader*
- *The Strange Story Of Juan Sousa's Zither*
- *Web Love*
- *The Neocons And The Jihadists: Hydra Of Unreason*
- *Unreality Television – Palimpsestual Textacy*
- *The Twelve Tasks Of Feldman*

No-nos – whatever you do, don't, in seriousness, write about how much you like Dan Brown's books. There's nothing wrong with them, they are perfectly serviceable hokey thrillers to pick up at an airport and read on a beach. But don't elevate them beyond that, you'll come across as the sort of person who gets excited at the announcement of a Maroon 5 tour. Which is a completely unnecessary undertaking on the part of band, audience, promoter and road crew.

HEROES
Don't list – your mum or dad (cheesy), Michael Jackson (or any other alleged celebrity sex offenders).

DETAILS
Status – just be honest. A friend of mine put 'swinger' for a joke, and got loads of dirty old men and rancid hags emailing for dates.

Here for – 'Networking' sounds a bit cold, 'Serious Relationship' sounds mental, so go with 'Dating' and 'Friends', it sounds relaxed and cool.

Religion – best to leave this blank. Another friend put 'Jihadist'. He's now been red-flagged on some kind of database.

Zodiac Sign – leave blank, no one in their right mind cares.

BLOG ENTRIES
If you're going to do a blog, make it interesting. Imagine you're actually writing for a newspaper, or an Internet news source. Do people really want to read your meanderings about whether Radiohead should do another *Bends* or

continue on their avant-garde exploration of the possibilities of rock-jazz-classical fusion? Here are some really uncool titles for Blog Entries:

- 'What I had for supper'
- 'Women I'd like to sleep with'
- 'Men who could turn me'
- 'iPod Love – A Modern Sonnet Sequence'
- 'Countries and races I don't like'
- 'My favourite episodes of *Dalziel and Pascoe*'
- 'Last night I heard my parents making love'
- 'The Problems Of Being A Writer In London OR How The City Stole My Muse'
- 'Girls needed for amateur porno'
- 'Glen Medeiros: A Reassessment'

BLURBS
About Me – Avoid the following:

- 'I'm crazy, me!'
- 'I like larging it!'

A note for the ladies – avoid putting things like 'I can be quite moody and tempestuous but, if you can put up with me, I'm worth it!' It doesn't make you sound like an intriguing challenge, it makes you sound like a high-maintenance egocentric bunny-boiling control freak.

Who I'd Like To Meet – This is the absolute worst type of uncool thing you can write:

> 'Everyone and anyone who wants to have FUN and meet people and DANCE and GO CRAZY!!!'

This is a fourteen-year-old's idea of cool. Piss off and learn chess.

This is almost as bad, in fact it might be worse because it's going for cool but overshoots painfully:

> 'All those who stand outside the global throttling of art as perpetrated by the blood-stained hands of the purse-string holders.'

That smacks of a card-carrying, tournament winning Grade-A Arsehole.

This is passable:

> 'Like-minded people who dig interesting stuff. I'm pretty chilled.'

But it's the sort of vacant nonsense by people who think having a poncho is the same thing as having a personality.

In truth, it's probably best to leave this section blank. After all, the really cool person is someone everyone else wants to meet. And who also doesn't prejudge others, and has a wide range of eclectic friends and acquaintances, acquired through their broad interests and non-judgemental social attitude.

COOL PLACES FOR WEEKEND BREAKS
Paris, Venice, Rome, New York.
UNCOOL PLACES FOR WEEKEND BREAKS
Peterborough, Plymouth, the northern seaboard of Russia, Hull.

LAUNCHING YOUR
COOL COOLOMETER TEST

1 You start a group on Facebook. Is it

a) The 'Fruit I Can Fit Up My Nostril' Group

b) The 'People Whose Heads I Would Display on the City Walls if I Was Mayor of London' Group

c) The 'Top Ten Bad Films You Secretly Like' Group

d) The 'Categories I'd Like to See in the Sex Olympics and Training I Will Give You for a Small Fee' Group

2 You start a blog on MySpace. You get no readers. Do you

a) Start fantasising about how to destroy the MySpace servers

b) Try to get attention by making politically provocative posts about the need to sterilise certain elements of society

c) Shrug it off

d) Send out messages to all the friends on your page about a great house party at '1A Bumhole Avenue, Wanktown'

3 Somebody sends you a message urging you to listen to a new band. Do you

a) Write back accusing them of stealing the songs from your dreams

b) Send them a film of yourself doing a nude dance to the tracks

c) Listen if you have time

d) Change your name to 'Johnnie Jackpot' and beg to be their manager

4 You are sent a friend request from someone you never liked at school on a social networking site. Do you

a) Send them a list of things you didn't like about them and a detailed list of fines for specific incidents

b) Stalk them till they have a breakdown

c) Either accept or reject them as a friend depending on the strength of your feeling

d) Write back suggesting a summit on neutral ground to hammer out a peace accord. Then if they turn up spray them with silly string and run away giggling in a high-pitched voice

5 Someone leaves a sexually suggestive comment about one of your photos. Do you

a) Leave one on theirs saying they look like they have a hideous genital infection

b) Try and sue them for a million pounds

c) Delete the comment if it makes you feel uncomfortable

d) Have the photo and the comment printed on a T-shirt, then hit the bars and clubs where you approach strangers by singing 'I've got a little something for you!'

If you answered mainly 'a', the world needs you like it needs a Steps comeback tour.

If you answered mainly 'b', you're so uncool that Darren Day drops your calls.

If you answered mainly 'c', get out there, you're cooler than Johnny Depp's fridge.

If you answered mainly 'd', you are about as cool as Gordon Brown stripping to Gary Glitter's 'I'm The Leader of the Gang (I Am)'.

Chapter 12
ONE STOP COOL SHOP

This last chapter is the 'Quick Start' section in the *How To Be Cool* manual. Just follow these instructions. Be warned, it does involve a bit of white lying. But that's because most people's jobs are spirit-crushingly boring. Now, obviously don't lie if you plan on meeting any of these people again. But if this is a one night hit of cool where you want to feel like the 50s Elvis in hoverboots, then use one of these:

MEN

You meet a woman at a bar. Buy her a drink and order yourself a

- Vodka martini, but say 'Stirred not shaken – James Bond is an amateur'
- Specific brand of malt whisky
- A glass of wine recommended by your uncle who owns a vineyard in the south of France
- DON'T ASK for the cheapest lager/blue WKD/ absinthe

When she asks what you do, say one of the following:

- 'I buy and sell yachts. Only come to London one week a year. I was thinking of selling the flat, but the Thames looks so beautiful at night.'
- 'I'm Ian McKellen's agent'
- 'I'm a lighting designer for U2'
- 'I work for a billionaire philanthropist distributing money to worthy causes'
- 'I designed the iPod'
- 'I'm a script reader for Steven Spielberg'
- 'I'm a jazz historian'
- DON'T SAY 'Wouldn't you like to know'/
  'Little bit of this, little bit of that'/
  'Why do you care? I'm just a piece of meat to you!'

She asks if you want to get some dinner. Say 'some other time' and give her your number, but say you can't that night because:

- You're babysitting your niece so your sister and her husband can go out for their anniversary
- You're going to a secret Paul McCartney gig, your cousin's his guitarist
- You have to go and support your best friend coming out to his parents
- It's the night you read stories at the local orphanage
- DON'T SAY 'Love to, but I forgot to skyplus *Rex Hunt's*

Fishing Adventures'/'Punching above our weight, aren't
we?'/'What have you got that my Xbox 360 hasn't?'

WOMEN

You meet a man at a bar. Buy him a drink and order
yourself a

- Glass of champagne
- Cocktail (NB anything except something you have a
  sneaking suspicion would be drunk by a social retard, i.e.
  ex-*EastEnders* star, beautician, Danielle Lloyd, etc.)
- A glass of wine recommended by this famous actor who
  owns a vineyard and is trying to get you into bed
- DON'T ASK for a vodka and Red Bull/Smirnoff Ice/flaming
  Sambuca

When he asks what you do, say one of the following:

- 'I do PR for Porsche'
- 'I'm a human rights lawyer'
- 'I play the cello in the London Symphony Orchestra.
  We're recording the soundtrack to the new Bond
  next week'
- 'I'm a lingerie designer'
- 'I'm researching a cure for a major disease'
- 'I manage a shop. You might have heard of it –
  Selfridges'

- DON'T SAY 'For fun or money?'/'I don't do the do, I'm not Betty Boo!'/'I Stack shelves at Woolworths, well I'm hoping the interview went pretty well!'

He asks if you want to get some dinner. Say 'some other time' and give him your number, but say you can't that night because:

- You're going to your friend's book launch at the British Museum
- Paxman's taking you out for dinner to persuade you to come and run his new production company
- You have to go to the new Pinter revival and write a review for a journalist friend who's sick and needs you to cover for them
- You promised your actors' agent sister you'd go to a party with her to check whether Jude Law really is serious about her or just flirting
- DON'T SAY 'I hear Steven Seagal's in town, I was going to try and get him to sign my copy of his album'/'Can I let you know in half an hour? I reckon, if I wait a bit longer, I can trade up on that offer'/'I have to finish my suduko book or bad things will happen'

CONCLUSION

So that's it! You're ready to get out there. No more feeling like a young Tory dancing out of time in the VIP section of a Status Quo gig. Now you can feel like Bono on stage at the Playboy Mansion! One more Coolometer question, and hopefully by now you don't need the answer: you'll know within you the path of cool you have to tread!

You rise to your feet to make a speech at your best friend's wedding. Do you

a) Perform your favourite farmyard impressions

b) Jump up on the table and mime to Britney Spears' 'Toxic'

c) Sparkle with wit and warmth so that everyone in the room wants you for their bride or groom

d) Perform a self-penned rap about the happy couple using samples from Billy Idol's 'White Wedding'

UNCOOL HATS

Top, bowler, one with fake birdshit and the logo 'Damn seagulls'

How to be Cool . . .

Now go for it! Turn heads, provoke smiles, get hearts racing. Before you know it, George Clooney will be wanting to be seen with you, and you'll be going 'Get away from me you loser, you're cramping my style!'

ACKNOWLEDGEMENTS

Thanks to my agent Antony Topping at Greene and Heaton, and to Rowan Yapp for coming to see the show and asking me to write the book.

Read more ...

Harry Thompson

PENGUINS STOPPED PLAY: Eleven Village Cricketers Take on the World

It seemed a simple enough idea at the outset: assemble a team of eleven men to play cricket on each of the seven continents of the globe

Except — hold on a minute — that's not a simple idea *at all*. And when you throw in incompetent airline officials, amorous Argentine colonels' wives, cunning Bajan drug dealers, gay Australian waiters, overzealous American anti-terrorist police, idiotic Welshmen dressed as Santa Claus, Archbishop Desmond Tutu and whole armies of pitch-invading Antarctic penguins, you quickly arrive at a whole lot more than you bargained for.

Harry Thompson's hilarious book tells the story of one of those great madcap enterprises that only an Englishman could have dreamed up, and only a bunch of Englishmen could possibly have wished to carry out.

'As funny as you'd expect from the writer of *Have I Got News For You*' *Daily Express*

'Rare, clever, creative . . . A maverick, pushing boundaries with outrageous jokes' *Guardian*

'Crammed with sharp observation, comic and cruel characterisation and a great many very good jokes . . . Gloriously funny and life-affirming' *Daily Telegraph*

Order your copy now by calling Bookpoint on 01235 827716 or visit your local bookshop quoting ISBN *978-0-7195-6346-1* *www.johnmurray.co.uk*

Read more ...

Michael Moran

SOD ABROAD: Why you'd be mad to leave the comfort of your own home

Ever written a postcard that says 'Wish we weren't here?'

Going on holiday? You must be mad. OK, it's not *absolutely* certain that you'll catch a fatal bout of food poisoning or be banged up in jail as a drugs mule. But you *might*. Why would a sane person risk it? Holidays aren't economical, they aren't ecological and they're not much bloody fun.

With travel tips, handy warnings and lists of stuff you can only do at home, *Sod Abroad* will help you kick the holiday habit. Instead, why not spend a fortnight on your sofa, in your home, watching your telly and eating food that you can actually pronounce?

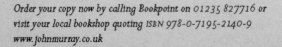
Order your copy now by calling Bookpoint on 01235 827716 or visit your local bookshop quoting ISBN 978-0-7195-2140-9
www.johnmurray.co.uk